1 MONTH OF FREE READING

at
www.ForgottenBooks.com

By purchasing this book you are eligible for one month membership to ForgottenBooks.com, giving you unlimited access to our entire collection of over 1,000,000 titles via our web site and mobile apps.

To claim your free month visit: www.forgottenbooks.com/free695281

* Offer is valid for 45 days from date of purchase. Terms and conditions apply.

English
Français
Deutsche
Italiano
Español
Português

www.forgottenbooks.com

Mythology Photography **Fiction** Fishing Christianity **Art** Cooking Essays Buddhism Freemasonry Medicine **Biology** Music **Ancient Egypt** Evolution Carpentry Physics Dance Geology **Mathematics** Fitness Shakespeare **Folklore** Yoga Marketing **Confidence** Immortality Biographies Poetry **Psychology** Witchcraft Electronics Chemistry History **Law** Accounting **Philosophy** Anthropology Alchemy Drama Quantum Mechanics Atheism Sexual Health **Ancient History Entrepreneurship** Languages Sport Paleontology Needlework Islam **Metaphysics** Investment Archaeology Parenting Statistics Criminology **Motivational**

1,000,000 Books

are available to read at

Forgotten Books

www.ForgottenBooks.com

Read online
Download PDF
Purchase in print

ISBN 978-1-334-28457-1
PIBN 10695281

This book is a reproduction of an important historical work. Forgotten Books uses state-of-the-art technology to digitally reconstruct the work, preserving the original format whilst repairing imperfections present in the aged copy. In rare cases, an imperfection in the original, such as a blemish or missing page, may be replicated in our edition. We do, however, repair the vast majority of imperfections successfully; any imperfections that remain are intentionally left to preserve the state of such historical works.

Forgotten Books is a registered trademark of FB &c Ltd.
Copyright © 2018 FB &c Ltd.
FB &c Ltd, Dalton House, 60 Windsor Avenue, London, SW19 2RR.
Company number 08720141. Registered in England and Wales.

For support please visit www.forgottenbooks.com

'THIS IS NOT THE TIME OR PLACE TO DO AS YOU DESIRE'

THE
STORY OF FRANCE

BY

MARY MACGREGOR

AUTHOR OF
"ROMANCE OF THE NETHERLANDS," "STORIES OF KING
ARTHUR'S KNIGHTS," "STORY OF JOHN RUSKIN"

WITH A FRONTISPIECE IN COLOR BY

WILLIAM RAINEY

NEW YORK
FREDERICK A. STOKES COMPANY
PUBLISHERS

'THIS IS NOT THE TIME OR PLACE TO DISCUSS OUR PRIVATE AFFAIRS.'

THE STORY OF FRANCE

BY

MARY MACGREGOR

AUTHOR OF
"ROMANCE OF THE NETHERLANDS," "STORIES OF KING
ARTHUR'S KNIGHTS," "STORY OF JOHN RUSKIN"

WITH A FRONTISPIECE IN COLOR BY

WILLIAM RAINEY

NEW YORK
FREDERICK A. STOKES COMPANY
PUBLISHERS

Copyright, 1920, by
FREDERICK A. STOKES COMPANY

All Rights Reserved

Printed in the United States of America

TO
CHRISTOPHER

CONTENTS

CHAP.		PAGE
I.	THE DRUIDS	1
II.	THE PATRIOT VERCINGETORIX	5
III.	KING ATTILA	12
IV.	THE FIRST KING OF FRANCE	17
V.	THE THREE LITTLE PRINCES	24
VI.	THE SLUGGARD KINGS	29
VII.	THE DEATH OF ST. BONIFACE	34
VIII.	ROLAND WINDS HIS HORN	40
IX.	LOUIS THE GOOD-NATURED	51
X.	THE VIKINGS	54
XI.	THE VIKINGS BESIEGE PARIS	59
XII.	ROLLO'S PRIDE	63
XIII.	KING ROBERT AND THE POPE	66
XIV.	THE TRUCE OF GOD	73
XV.	PETER THE HERMIT	77
XVI.	THE ORIFLAMME	87
XVII.	THE SECOND CRUSADE	92
XVIII.	ARTHUR, PRINCE OF NORMANDY, DISAPPEARS	99
XIX.	THE BATTLE OF BOUVINES	104
XX.	THE VOW OF ST. LOUIS	110
XXI.	ST. LOUIS IS TAKEN PRISONER	115

CONTENTS

CHAP.		PAGE
XXII.	THE SICILIAN VESPERS	122
XXIII.	THE BATTLE OF THE SPURS	126
XXIV.	POPE BONIFACE TAKEN PRISONER	131
XXV.	THE SALIC LAW	136
XXVI.	THE BATTLE OF SLUYS	140
XXVII.	THE BATTLE OF CRÉCY	145
XXVIII.	THE SIEGE OF CALAIS	151
XXIX.	THE BATTLE OF POITIERS	157
XXX.	THE REBELLION OF JACQUES	163
XXXI.	SIR BERTRAND DU GUESCLIN	167
XXXII.	THE BATTLE OF ROOSEBEK	175
XXXIII.	THE MAD KING	181
XXXIV.	THE TWO LILY PRINCES	185
XXXV.	THE BATTLE OF AGINCOURT	189
XXXVI.	THE BABY-KING OF FRANCE	194
XXXVII.	THE SIEGE OF ORLEANS	199
XXXVIII.	JOAN SEES THE DAUPHIN	203
XXXIX.	JOAN RELIEVES ORLEANS	210
XL.	JOAN LEADS THE DAUPHIN TO RHEIMS	216
XLI.	THE DEATH OF THE MAID	221
XLII.	THE LEAGUE OF THE COMMON WEAL	225
XLIII.	LOUIS XI. VISITS CHARLES THE BOLD	230
XLIV.	THE DEATH OF CHARLES THE BOLD	236
XLV.	MADAME LA GRANDE	242
XLVI.	BAYARD IS TAKEN PRISONER	248
XLVII.	BAYARD HOLDS THE BRIDGE ALONE	254
XLVIII.	THE FIELD OF THE CLOTH OF GOLD	259

CONTENTS

CHAP.		PAGE
XLIX.	THE DEATH OF BAYARD	266
L.	THE REFORMERS	271
LI.	THE "GABELLE" OR SALT TAX	275
LII.	THE SIEGE OF ST. QUENTIN	278
LIII.	THE PRINCE OF CONDÉ TAKEN PRISONER	282
LIV.	THE PRINCE OF CONDÉ KILLED	288
LV.	ADMIRAL COLIGNY GOES TO PARIS	294
LVI.	ST. BARTHOLOMEW'S DAY	297
LVII.	HENRY OF NAVARRE ESCAPES FROM PARIS	302
LVIII.	THE KING OF PARIS	306
LIX.	THE PRINCE OF BÉARN	311
LX.	RAVAILLAC STABS THE KING	317
LXI.	THE ITALIAN FAVORITE	323
LXII.	THE SIEGE OF LA ROCHELLE	328
LXIII.	THE DAY OF DUPES	333
LXIV.	THE WARS OF THE FRONDE	339
LXV.	THE DILIGENT KING	345
LXVI.	LOUIS XIV. PERSECUTES THE HUGUENOTS	351
LXVII.	THE BREAD OF THE PEASANTS	356
LXVIII.	THE TAKING OF QUEBEC	362
LXIX.	MARIE ANTOINETTE	370
LXX.	THE TAKING OF THE BASTILLE	376
LXXI.	THE FISHWIVES AT VERSAILLES	381
LXXII.	THE FLIGHT OF THE ROYAL FAMILY	387
LXXIII.	LOUIS XVI. IS EXECUTED	392
LXXIV.	MARIE ANTOINETTE IS EXECUTED	397
LXXV.	NAPOLEON BONAPARTE	402

CONTENTS

CHAP.		PAGE
LXXVI.	THE BRIDGE OF LODI	408
LXXVII.	THE BATTLE OF THE PYRAMIDS	413
LXXVIII.	THE GREAT ST. BERNARD PASS	417
LXXIX.	THE "SUN OF AUSTERLITZ"	421
LXXX.	THE BERLIN DECREE	427
LXXXI.	THE RETREAT FROM MOSCOW	431
LXXXII.	NAPOLEON IS BANISHED TO ELBA	436
LXXXIII.	THE BATTLE OF WATERLOO	439
LXXXIV.	THE REVOLUTION OF JULY	444
LXXXV.	THE BRAVE ARCHBISHOP	448
LXXXVI.	THE SIEGE OF SEBASTOPOL	452
LXXXVII.	"THE MAN OF SEDAN"	455
LXXXVIII.	THE THIRD REPUBLIC	459
LXXXIX.	GROWTH OF DEMOCRACY	469
XC.	THE COMING OF THE GREAT WAR	476
XCI.	FOUR YEARS OF FIGHTING	485
XCII.	VICTORY	494
	LIST OF KINGS	499
	INDEX	503

THE STORY OF FRANCE

CHAPTER I

THE DRUIDS

Long, long ago the land which we now call France was called Gaul.

Gaul was much larger than France is to-day, although north, south, and west France has the same boundaries now as Gaul had in the far-off days of which I am going to tell you.

What these boundaries are, many a geography lesson will have shown. But, lest you have forgotten, take a map of Europe, and you will see that on the north France has to protect her the English Channel, on the south she is guarded by the Mediterranean and the Pyrenees, while on her west roll the waters of the Atlantic. These mountains and waters were also the bulwarks of ancient Gaul.

It was on the east that Gaul stretched far beyond the boundaries of France, reaching to the Alps and to the swift-flowing river Rhine.

And it is of Gaul, as it was in those far-off days many centuries B.C., that I wish first to tell you.

The large tract of land called Gaul was then little more than a dreary waste of moor and marsh, with great forests, larger and gloomier than any you have ever seen.

Through these forests and marshlands terrible beasts prowled—wolves, bears, wild oxen. Herds of swine, too, fierce as any wolves, roamed through the marshes. These had been tamed enough to answer to their keeper's horn.

As for the people who lived in Gaul in those days, they were almost as savage as the wild beasts. Half naked, they too, like the wolves and bears, wandered through the marshes and forests to seek for food.

They were tall and strong, these huntsmen, with blue eyes and yellow hair. If you had met a savage Gallic warrior, you would have thought he looked wild and fierce enough to frighten any foe. But, you know, people do not often see themselves as others see them. That is why the Scottish poet Burns sang—

> "O wad some Power the giftie gie us
> To see oursels as ithers see us."

These warriors with blue eyes and yellow hair thought that they did not look at all fierce, and so they would often stain their yellow locks red, to make themselves appear, as they thought, terrible to their foes.

Although they wore few clothes, the Gauls were fond of ornaments, and often they adorned themselves with heavy chains and collars of gold.

Stalwart warriors as well as huntsmen were these yellow-haired men. Different tribes or clans, led each by his own chief, would hunt one another and fight to the death.

In these far-off days the clans often fought to win a piece of land on which another clan had settled and built huts. It is true that the huts were rough and comfortless, yet they were the only shelter these wild folk knew from the storm and cold. Very often, too, it was bitterly cold. In winter the rivers were frozen for weeks at a time. They were frozen so hard that they were used as highways, and heavy wagons with great loads could be rolled or drawn across the solid ice without a fear that it would give way.

The Gauls built their huts of wood and clay, covering them with straw and with branches cut from the great

THE DRUIDS

trees of the forests. They were huddled close together, and round them the Gauls threw up a rough wall of timber, earth, stone. This wall was meant to protect the town or encampment, as it was called, from the attacks of an unfriendly tribe.

Yet when the war-cry was heard drawing nearer and nearer to the little settlement, the people, after all, did not always wait to defend their town.

It was so simple to build other huts, that sometimes, at the sound of the terrible war-whoop, the whole clan would flee for greater safety into the depths of the forests.

Here, to be ready for such a flight, they had already felled trees, which they now set to work, in grim earnest, to pile up into an enormous barricade between themselves and the foe that was all the while drawing near.

After the battle was over, the victorious clan held a great feast, to which they brought the prisoners whom they had taken in the fight. While their victors danced wild dances and shouted triumphant war-songs, the poor prisoners looked on with sullen faces and with heavy hearts, for well they knew what would now befall them.

They would be tied to trees and burned, or, if they escaped that cruel fate, it would perhaps be to be flogged to death. Their conquerors were pitiless, the prisoners knew it well. They might even be sacrificed to the gods. For the Gauls never doubted that their gods demanded human sacrifices.

But though the tribes which wandered now here, now there, throughout the land of Gaul were wild and warlike, yet already they had priests to whom they yielded obedience as well as reverence.

These priests were called Druids. You have read of Druids in the early history of your own land, and you may have seen some of the temples in which they worshiped long years ago. The temples were but simple circles of stones, open to the blue sky and fresh winds of heaven.

These stones are still to be seen in England and in the west of France.

Usually the Druids were grave old men with long white beards, who were believed to be very wise. They were not often seen, for they dwelt in the depths of some sacred wood, where, silent and alone, they sought to learn the will of their gods.

But once every year the Druids, clad in their long white robes, with sickles in their hands, would summon the wandering tribes together, and go with them into the forest. There, under the oak trees, they would gather. The trees themselves were cold and bare, but they were sacred, and upon them grew the mistletoe with its green leaves and pure white berries.

The mistletoe as well as the oak was sacred to the gods, and with their sickles the priests cut it down and carried it in triumph to their temples.

The Druids were not only the teachers of the people, they were also their poets and priests. It was from them that the Gauls learned to sacrifice their prisoners to the gods.

From the Druids, also, the Gallic warriors heard that when they were slain in battle, they would live again in some other world the same life that they had lived on earth.

When they heard this, the warriors said, "In this other world we must have our slaves, our horses and our dogs, to wait upon us as they have done here. Our swords and our shields, also, we will not leave behind us."

Thus it was that when a great warrior was buried, his slave, his horse, his dog, each was buried alive with his master. His sword and shield also were not forgotten. And the white-robed Druids who ruled the Gauls in these olden days, though they had the power, did not forbid this cruel rite.

CHAPTER II

THE PATRIOT VERCINGETORIX

As I have told you, different tribes in Gaul fought one with the other. But sometimes the clans forgot their own quarrels, that they might join together against a common foe. Feeling that even then they were not strong enough, they would appeal to Rome to help them against the fierce German warriors, who poured across the river Rhine and invaded Gaul.

These Germans, when they were victorious, treated their prisoners even more cruelly than the Gauls treated each other.

It was natural that the Gallic chiefs should ask the Romans to help them, for the Romans were a strong people, with well-disciplined legions of soldiers. Already, too, they had a special interest in Gaul, as their provinces were scattered up and down the country.

Long before this, in 283 B.C., a few Roman families, led by three Roman officers, journeyed to a part of Gaul called Cisalpine Gaul. Here they took possession of some ground on the borders of the Adriatic Sea. On the ground they planted the standard of Rome, a golden eagle, which they had carried before them on their journey.

The officers ordered a round hole to be dug, and in this hole they laid a handful of earth and a cluster of fruit, which, along with the standard, they had brought from Rome.

Taking a plow, and yoking to it a white bull and a white heifer, the settlers then drew a furrow round a large piece of ground, after which the bull and the heifer were sacrificed to the gods of Rome, and the ceremony was complete.

Thus the first Roman colony was planted in Gaul. Fifteen years passed and another Roman colony was founded, with the same rites, and then another and another. And wherever the Romans went, they drained the land and built houses, bridges, towns.

Many of the Gauls among whom they dwelt learned to copy these Roman buildings, which were so much better than their own rude huts and irregular villages.

The first time a Roman army came to Gaul, it was led by a great general, called Scipio, and landed about 218 B.C. at Massilia, which in those long-ago days was the name for Marseilles.

Massilia opened its gates to the Romans, and welcomed them to its city, which was already an ancient one, having been founded by a Greek, 600 B.C.

More than a hundred years after the Romans had settled at Massilia, a terrible earthquake startled the inhabitants of northern Europe. A fierce German tribe, feeling no longer safe in the north, began to travel southward, and never stopped until it reached Gaul.

Crossing the Rhone, the barbarians came to the camp of Marius, a Roman general.

They at once offered to fight, but Marius paid no heed to the taunts by which they tried to rouse him, and allowed them to pass on their way.

Some time later he broke up his camp and followed the invaders. He found them, among the mountains, not far from the town of Aix. Here, in 102 B.C., Marius fought with the rude Germans and defeated them with terrible slaughter.

The victory of Aix was an important one; for had the barbarians conquered, they would probably have gone on to Italy to try to vanquish Rome. Thus they might have become the masters of the world.

THE PATRIOT VERCINGETORIX 7

Two years after this victory, the man who was to succeed Marius was born. This was Julius Cæsar, one of the greatest and most ambitious generals of Rome.

For years Gaul suffered from the invasion of the Germans. But when, in the year 62 B.C., great hordes of these warriors poured across the Rhine, more than ever determined to wrest the land from its owners, the Gauls turned again to Rome, begging for help.

The Romans, eager to keep their own colonies, perhaps also eager for new conquests, sent Julius Cæsar, who was now a man thirty-eight years of age, to the aid of the Gauls.

Even by the well-disciplined troops of Rome the Germans were not easily beaten, but at length Cæsar utterly routed them, and they fled in confusion toward the Rhine, anxious only to go back to their own land.

Now that they were delivered from their foes, the Gauls would gladly have seen the brave Roman warriors march back to Rome. But the Romans did not mean to go away, as the Gauls very soon found out. They meant to stay until they were themselves masters of Gaul.

This was no light task, for the Gauls dearly loved their independence. At the end of six years, though some tribes had been forced to submit, the struggle against Cæsar was in reality fiercer than it had ever been.

Their country was in danger, and the Gauls, forgetting their own quarrels, determined to unite against their foe in one last great attempt to win freedom for themselves and their country.

A young Gaul was the chief leader of the revolt. His real name is not known, but in history he is always called Vercingetorix, which means "chief of a hundred kings."

Vercingetorix belonged to a powerful tribe, and Cæsar, with his usual wisdom, had tried to win the young chief over to his side. But he had failed. And now, about 53 B.C., Vercingetorix had come down from the mountains with his followers and seized Gergovia, the capital of his tribe and his own birthplace.

The Gauls flocked to his standard. But whether love drew them or fear, it is difficult to tell, for Vercingetorix had decreed that whoever stayed away should be punished with torture or with death.

Cæsar was in Italy when the rebellion led by the young Gaul broke out, but he no sooner heard of it than he hastened back to Gaul, and put himself at the head of his well-trained legions.

Vercingetorix knew he could not hope to destroy the Roman legions in the open field, but he could attack small bands of the enemy and harass their movements.

Moreover, he begged the people of Gaul to destroy their dwellings, their springs, their bridges, their provisions, so that when Cæsar came he might find nothing but ruins.

But in spite of all that Vercingetorix could do, Cæsar reached Gergovia, and at once laid siege to the town, which was really a rough cluster of huts, surrounded by strong barricades made out of trunks of trees.

The Gauls were not used to be shut up in a town, and soon they were clamoring to be led against the enemy.

But Cæsar had seen tribe after tribe joining the young Gallic chief. One of his legions, too, when ordered to assault the walls of Gergovia, had been driven back with the loss of forty-six of its bravest officers, and Cæsar thought it was time to raise the siege.

The Gauls could scarcely believe their eyes when they saw the Roman army withdrawing. It was the first time that Cæsar had been unable to take a Gallic town, and the Gauls, shouting in triumph, declared that their foe was vanquished. Vercingetorix himself believed it would now be well to strike a blow at the enemy, and placing himself at the head of his followers, he led them against the retreating army. Within nine miles of the fugitives he pitched his

THE PATRIOT VERCINGETORIX

camp, and gathering together his chiefs he spoke to them these proud words:

"Now is the hour of victory; the Romans are flying to their province and leaving Gaul; that is enough for our liberty to-day, but too little for the peace and repose of the future; for they will return with greater armies, and the war will be without end."

Then the young Gaul ordered his troops to pursue the retreating foe. He did not know that Cæsar had added to his army a large number of horsemen from the fierce German tribes which were still wandering through the country, and had promised them lands and plunder, as well as wages, if they proved faithful.

Now the battle began. One band of Gauls seized a road by which the Romans must pass, hoping to bar their passage. While the fight raged fiercely at this point, the wild German horsemen dashed up a height held by the Gauls, drove them away, and chased them toward a river where Vercingetorix was stationed.

Cæsar ordered his legion to attack the Gauls as they fled toward their leader, and soon the fugitives dashed in among Vercingetorix's company followed by the Romans. The Gallic army was in utter confusion.

With great difficulty Vercingetorix rallied his men and ordered a retreat. The Roman general followed, taking many prisoners, and killing more than three thousand Gauls.

Vercingetorix succeeded in reaching a town called Alesia, and with the remnant of his army he at once began to fortify the place.

As you may imagine, Julius Cæsar had soon followed the Gauls to Alesia. When he saw them within the walls of the town, he determined to keep them there. He ordered his great army at once to surround the town and begin to dig trenches and build forts to keep the Gauls from escaping.

Again and again Vercingetorix tried to destroy the

Roman forts and trenches, but each time he was beaten back into Alesia.

But the young Gaul had a brave spirit, and he still hoped to win the day. One night, by his orders, some Gallic horsemen stole quietly and unnoticed through the Roman lines, and hastened each to his own tribe to summon it to arms.

Before long the Gauls throughout the country were roused and galloping to the help of Vercingetorix.

And so it happened that one day the Romans were surprised and attacked in their entrenchments by a new army of Gauls.

A terrible struggle followed. Each time the new Gallic army attacked the enemy, Vercingetorix led his men out of the gates of Alesia and joined in the assault.

The Romans fought desperately. To be beaten by these rough, untrained warriors would humble their pride in the dust.

The Gauls, too, strained every nerve to win. To be beaten by the Roman legions would mean the loss of home, of country, of freedom.

For four days the battle raged, and then at length the well-trained troops of Rome were victorious.

The Gallic army had been cut to pieces, and Vercingetorix and a few men pushed back into Alesia. Escape was now impossible.

Then Vercingetorix, with rare courage, offered to give himself up to the Romans, that his followers might go free, and not one voice was raised to bid him stay.

Too heedless of his life, now that his country was lost, the young Gaul did not wait to send before him a herald of peace.

Mounting his war-horse, he rode away alone into Cæsar's camp, and found the great general seated on his tribunal to give judgment.

Dismounting in silence, Vercingetorix threw his weapons

THE PATRIOT VERCINGETORIX

at the feet of his conqueror; then flinging himself down beside them, he pleaded for mercy.

But Julius Cæsar had no pity. Rome's stern motto was "Vae Victis," Woe to the vanquished!

Vercingetorix was loaded with chains and taken to Rome. For six long years he was there in a dungeon.

Then, when Cæsar came to Rome to give thanks to the gods for his victories, Vercingetorix was led, with other prisoners, in the triumphal procession. Afterwards he was taken back to his dungeon and beheaded.

After Vercingetorix had given himself up to Cæsar the war still dragged on, but without their young chief the Gauls fought ever more and more listlessly. By the end of the year 51 B.C. the country was subdued. Cæsar treated the conquered people kindly, and even enrolled among his own troops Gauls whose bravery he had proved.

One legion, too, he formed almost wholly of the conquered people, calling it the "Alauda" or "Lark." For on their helmets the soldiers of this legion had engraved the figure of a lark, the old Gallic symbol of wakefulness.

CHAPTER III

KING ATTILA

For five centuries Gaul was now ruled by the Romans. The people hated their conquerors, for they were forced to pay them taxes, and until now, 50 B.C., they had been free, owing obedience to none. Taxes were to them the sign of their bondage.

Yet the Romans were not cruel to the people they had conquered. Indeed, they taught them many useful things, so that gradually the people became less wild and savage. Instead of mud huts they learned to build comfortable houses, and soon they possessed cities of which they were proud. They drained the dreary marshlands, made good roads and built bridges. They even dressed as did their conquerors, and spoke their language.

Many of the great forests, too, were cut down, and thus the wild beasts gradually disappeared, so that, instead of wild hogs, quiet sheep were to be seen browsing in the fields.

You remember that the winters in Gaul were bitterly cold. Now, as the forests were gradually cut down, the rays of the sun reached the earth and warmed it, so that the weather grew less severe.

In the south of Gaul the Romans then began to plant vines. These took root and spread, so that when Gaul became France the vine was already known all over the southern part of the country. Olives, too, began to be cultivated, and the olive crops were soon as valuable as the corn crops.

Finding that the Druids, those mysterious white-robed priests, encouraged the Gauls to offer human sacrifices, the Romans banished them from the land. But while the Romans did their utmost to stamp out the ancient Druidical worship, in later years they brought to the Gauls a new religion, for about the year 244 A.D. Rome sent seven bishops into Gaul.

Little by little the Gospel spread among the fierce Gallic warriors, moving them sometimes to love and always to wonder, so strangely in their ears rang the tidings of peace and goodwill to man.

About seven years after the bishops reached Gaul, a church was founded at Paris, which in these far-off days was called Lutetia.

Lutetia had already become the capital of northern Gaul, and from this city the Christian religion began in 251 A.D. to spread rapidly all over the land.

Meanwhile the power of the Romans was growing less and less. And the wild barbarian tribes across the Rhine thought that now was the time to sweep down upon Gaul, and wrench her from the nation whose legions they had been used to fear.

The Germans, as these wild tribes were named, were in appearance much like the Gallic tribes they had come to conquer.

For the Germans had blue eyes and long yellow hair like the Gauls, although they were much taller than they, while over the Romans they towered like giants.

But while the Gauls wore bright colors and adorned themselves with ornaments, the Germans were content to wear only a rough skin, which they fastened round their bodies with a skewer or pin.

In other ways, too, the tribes were unlike each other, in spite of blue eyes and yellow hair.

The Gauls were ever ready to talk, to tell of their wonderful deeds, which deeds had not always taken place;

for the Gaul's imagination was as vivid as the clothes he liked to wear.

The Germans did not boast, indeed they talked but little. Yet they were determined and constant, and seldom failed in what they set their will to do.

In their home life, too, the Gauls and Germans had different customs. One of these was that the Gauls were served by slaves, whom they treated as they treated their beasts, while those who waited on the Germans sat round the hearths of their masters, and were treated as friends and comrades.

Three chief German tribes overran Gaul—the Visigoths, the Burgundians, and the Franks.

Julian, the Roman emperor, in 355 A.D. found that all his strength was needed to fight the Franks, who were the most powerful of the three German tribes. In spite of all he could do, however, northern Gaul was soon seized and held by these wild ambitious Germans.

The emperor therefore went himself to the north, and set up his court at Paris, or Lutetia, as this small village, built on a little island in the river Seine, was then called. He hoped by his presence to subdue the Franks.

But his hope was vain, and in 357 A.D. Lutetia itself, which Julian loved for its sea breezes and its vines and figs, was filled with Franks, and the emperor was forced to admit them to his court, and even to employ them in his army.

So great became the power of these persistent Franks, that in 387 A.D. Argobast, one of their chiefs, became Emperor of the West in all but name. The real emperor was Theodosius, but Argobast was powerful enough to put his own followers into every position of trust in the kingdom.

When Theodosius died, his successor Valentinian was determined to get rid of Argobast. He thought it would be a simple matter to depose the Frank, and himself handed him a writ or paper, bidding him give up all claim to the imperial throne.

With true Frankish scorn for his enemy, Argobast tore up the writ, trampled it beneath his feet in the presence of Valentinian, and then went on his way as before.

When, a short time after this, Valentinian was strangled as he slept, Argobast put Eugenius, who had been a schoolmaster, on the emperor's seat. He himself took the highest position next to the emperor, being called a "Mayor of the Palace."

In 394 A.D. Argobast, who was a pagan, led the emperor's forces to battle against the Christians in Gaul.

Eugenius, who himself was on the battlefield, was killed and his army utterly defeated. Then Argobast, fearing that he might be captured and slain by the enemy, fell upon his sword and died.

In northern Gaul the Franks were now more powerful than the Romans. In the south the Visigoths and Burgundians, the other great German tribes, had made a home for themselves, and were living more or less peaceably among the Romans and Gauls. The country might therefore soon have been at peace, but in 450 A.D. a barbarous people called the Huns invaded the land. The Huns came from the east, where they had already laid waste country and town. They had no wish to conquer Gaul and settle in it. All they cared for was to conquer and destroy.

The Huns were led by their king, Attila, who was so cruel that he was named "The Scourge of God."

Against so dread a foe all the different tribes in Gaul united, being led by Theodoric, a Visigoth, and Aëtius, a Roman general. It was a conflict on which much depended, for should the Huns conquer Gaul they would attack Spain, Italy and finally rule over the whole western world.

Meanwhile, in the summer of 451 A.D., Attila besieged Orleans. The town was considered sacred in those days and was called Aureliacum.

For a time the city held out bravely, but at length the bishop sent a message to Aëtius, saying, "If thou be not here this very day, my son, it will be too late."

Yet still Aëtius did not come, and Orleans was forced to surrender. As the Huns began to plunder the city, however, loud shouts rent the air. Aëtius and Theodoric had come at last. They fell upon the Huns so fiercely that Attila was forced to retreat.

At length they reached the plains of Châlons-sur-Marne. Aëtius and Theodoric, who had followed, were now close behind. Attila ordered his men to halt. He was determined to fight and overthrow the bold Roman, the undaunted Visigoth, who had forced him to leave Orleans, his hardly won prize.

On the plains of Châlons-sur-Marne a terrible battle then began. All afternoon and evening the struggle lasted. Theodoric was slain, and when night came those who had fallen were too many to be numbered.

Aëtius and his followers were victorious. Attila, expecting that his camp would be attacked, made ready a great funeral-pyre on which he meant to die rather than be captured by the Romans and Franks. But Aëtius was worn out after the battle, and the Huns were free to retreat across the Rhine. Thus the country was saved from King Attila and his barbarous followers.

Gaul was now no longer a province of Rome. The German tribes had gradually taken possession of the country. Rome, indeed, had fallen on such evil days, that she soon ceased to have an emperor of her own. Even as her first emperor was a Romulus, so was her last, who in 476 A.D. was deposed. There was now no Emperor of the West, the Emperor of the East ruling supreme from the Bosphorus, until the year 800 A.D., when, as you shall hear, Charles the Great became the head of the Holy Roman Empire with the title "Emperor of Rome."

CHAPTER IV

THE FIRST KING OF FRANCE

AMONG the Franks who had settled in northern Gaul, the Salian Franks were the strongest. The heads of the Salian Franks were called Merwings or Merovingians.

It is said that Meroveus, one of these Merwings, was a sea-king, and you will remember his name because the kings of his race were called after him the Merovingians.

Meroveus had long yellow hair reaching to his shoulders, so the kings of his line always wore their hair long. Indeed, one of the titles of the Frankish kings was "Long-Haired." By degrees these long locks became a sign of royalty; to have them shorn a token of disgrace.

Whether Meroveus was really a sea-king or not, his son Childeric was certainly king of the Salian Franks, and died in 481 A.D., leaving his son Clovis, a boy of fifteen, to succeed him.

Clovis might not have become king because he was Childeric's son, but the lad had already shown on the battlefield that he was strong and could be brave. The warriors of his tribe therefore chose him, by vote, to be their king. To let the people know on whom their choice had fallen they placed Clovis on their shields and carried him thus through their towns and villages.

At fifteen years of age the lad was king of only a small tribe of Salian Franks; by the time he was forty-five years of age he had won all Gaul for himself and his Frankish warriors.

The only Roman governor left in northern Gaul when

Clovis became king was Syagrius. He was rash enough to proclaim himself prince of the province of Soissons.

But the young king of the Franks would have no Roman, or, for the matter of that, no Frank either, ruling in opposition to him. He called his warriors together in 486 A.D. and declared war against Syagrius. Then shouting their fierce battle-cry, clashing their iron javelins upon their great white shields, the Franks set out to fight the Roman.

Syagrius did his utmost to defend his province, but neither skill nor strength was of any use before the furious onslaught of the Franks. The Roman governor was taken and secretly put to death, while Clovis established his capital at Soissons.

This success roused the ambition of Clovis. He sent his warriors out all over the country, bidding them lay waste those provinces that refused to own him as their lord.

In this way Gaul was gradually won for the king of the Franks, and the country which was ruled by the king of the Franks now, in 496 A.D., began to be known as France.

As the king's kingdom grew larger, his power also became greater. Before long it was plain that Clovis meant to use his power.

The king was a pagan, that is, he worshiped idols, as did also his followers. But, as you know, the Romans had brought the teaching of Christ to Gaul, and here and there churches had been built in which to worship Him. These churches were already rich and held many treasures.

Clovis, being a pagan, did not hesitate to enter the churches and seize their treasures, whenever there was an opportunity to do so.

There was a law among the Franks, that all the booty taken in war should be equally divided among the warriors, the king taking his share by lot, as did the others.

THE FIRST KING OF FRANCE

One day Clovis's warriors came to a town called Rheims. Here there was a church which contained, among other treasures, a beautiful vase. It was said to be "of marvelous size and beauty." The soldiers did not fear to add the vase to their booty.

The Bishop of Rheims had sent his good wishes to Clovis when he was chosen king, and Clovis had been pleased with the priest's kindness.

When the bishop heard that the church at Rheims had been sacked, and that the vase had been carried away, he sent a messenger to the king, begging that all the church's treasures might be sent back, but if that could not be, that at least the vase "of marvelous size and beauty" should be returned.

Clovis, pagan though he was, wished to please the bishop, and bade the messenger go with him to Soissons, where the booty was to be divided.

When they reached the capital, the plunder was piled up in a great heap, and round it stood the host commanded by the king.

Clovis, determined to please the bishop, stepped forward and said, "Valiant warriors, I pray thee not to refuse me, over and above my share, this vase," and he pointed to the one which the bishop valued so greatly.

The Franks, who were proud of their king because he led them always to victory, answered his appeal right royally.

"Glorious king," they cried, "everything we see here is thine, and we ourselves are submissive to thy command. Do thou as seemeth good to thee, for there is none that can resist thy power."

You can imagine how pleased Clovis was as he listened to the words of his brave warriors.

But among these warriors was one who thought it would be a fine thing to defy his king. He broke from the ranks and struck the beautiful vase with his battle-ax, so that it was broken in half. Then pointing to the pile of booty, he shouted, "Thou shalt have naught of all this, O king, save what the lots shall truly give thee."

Clovis took no notice of the soldier's rudeness. It seemed as though he had not heard, for he took the broken vase and gave it to the bishop's messenger.

But punishment was yet to be meted out to the insolent soldier. Some months later, Clovis ordered his battle host to assemble, that he might, as was his custom, inspect their arms. All went well until the king came to the soldier who had struck the vase.

Before him the king lingered, looking at his lance, his sword, his battle-ax. Then stern and loud he spoke: "None hath brought hither arms so ill-kept as thine, nor lance, nor sword, nor battle-ax are fit for service"; and snatching the battle-ax from the soldier's hand, Clovis flung it to the ground.

As the warrior stooped to pick it up, the king seized his own battle-ax, swung it high above his head, and bringing it down upon the soldier's neck, said, "Thus diddest thou to the vase at Soissons."

Rough as the times were, the king's deed filled his warriors with fear.

Now as Clovis journeyed through his land, he heard of a beautiful princess named Clotilde. Clotilde was a Christian, yet Clovis, the worshiper of idols, determined to marry her.

The bishops and priests were pleased that Clovis should marry Clotilde. They thought that for the love he bore his wife the king would soon become a Christian, and the bishops wished the powerful young monarch to be on their side. When the priests told Clovis the story of Christ's death upon the Cross, he cried, "Had I and my Franks been there we would have avenged the wrong."

Clotilde also longed to see her husband give up his idols, and often she would plead with him to pray to the true

THE FIRST KING OF FRANCE

God. But the years passed, and still Clovis clung to his idols.

At length the queen had a little son. She begged Clovis to let their child be baptized by the Bishop of Rheims. Perhaps in her heart she hoped that Clovis would himself be baptized with his boy.

Ofttimes she said to the king, "The gods you worship are naught and can do naught for themselves or others: they are of wood or stone or metal."

Clovis loved Clotilde well, and although he was not yet willing to give up his gods, he could not refuse to let their little son be baptized as Clotilde wished. So the bishop came to the palace, and the child was baptized in the name of Christ.

The queen was glad, and looked more beautiful than ever in her joy. But in a little while her joy faded, for her little son grew ill and died.

To add to Clotilde's grief Clovis reproached her. In his pain he scarce knew what he said.

"Had the child been dedicated to my gods he would have been alive," he muttered. "He was baptized in the name of your God and could not live."

Clotilde answered gently, "I bear up against my sorrow, because I believe in the wisdom and goodness of the true God. Our little babe is with the whitest angels in heaven."

Then Clovis grew ashamed and silent before the patience of Clotilde. When another little son was born he also was baptized, and as he grew strong and lusty, Clovis began to think more kindly of Christ.

Now, soon after the birth of his second son, a fierce German tribe attacked the Franks. Clovis at once set out to punish the invaders. When he had said good-by to his wife she had begged him, once again, to give up his strange gods. But on the eve of battle how dare he forsake those who had often given him victory? So he had closed his heart against Clotilde's words.

In the midst of the battle Clovis saw that his soldiers were beginning to waver before the fury of the enemy.

At that moment one of his servants also saw that the battle was going against his master. Then he called out, so says an old chronicler, "My lord king, believe only on the Lord of Heaven, whom the queen my mistress preacheth."

Then in his despair Clovis raised his hands and prayed, "Christ Jesus, Thou whom my Queen Clotilde calleth the Son of the living God, I have invoked my own gods and they have withdrawn from me. . . . Thee, very God and Lord, I invoke; if Thou give me victory over these foes . . . I will believe on Thee and be baptized in Thy name."

Shouting his war-cry anew, Clovis once again led his men against the foe, and lo! the victory was his.

When Clotilde heard how the battle had been won, she was glad, but gladder still she grew as the day drew near on which her lord would be baptized.

From the palace to the church the royal procession walked when the great day dawned, the bishop leading the king by the hand as a little child. Following the king came the queen, more joyous than on her bridal morn, while behind her pressed the people. They, too, were going to be baptized with Clovis.

So great was the splendor prepared for the royal procession that, as he passed along the road from the palace to the church, the king said to the bishop, "Father, is not this itself that heaven which you have promised me?"

With Clovis were baptized three thousand of his warriors, as well as many women and children.

After his baptism the king went back to his wars, for he could not rest until he had brought all Gaul under his own rule. But now, when he went forth to battle, Clovis no longer invoked his old gods of wood and stone; instead, he prayed to one of the saints of the Christian Church.

Soon after he became a Christian, Clovis went to Paris. And there, in the city which the Emperor Julian had loved

THE FIRST KING OF FRANCE

for its sea breezes, its vines and figs, Clovis established his capital.

The work of the king was now nearly over. But before he died, Clovis confessed all the evil he had done, and knowing that he had often been cruel and unjust, he said that he had need of a "large pardon."

It was in the gray autumn days of the year 511 A.D. that King Clovis died at Paris, and was buried in a church which had been built by his wife Clotilde.

And you will remember that to Clovis belongs the glory of founding the kingdom of France, and of making it a Christian land.

CHAPTER V

THE THREE LITTLE PRINCES

After the death of Clovis, northern France was divided among his four sons.

One of these died, leaving behind him three little boys, who lived with their grandmother Clotilde. The little princes loved their grandmother, and were as happy as three little boys could be.

One day a messenger came to Queen Clotilde from two of her sons, Clotair and Hildebert, saying, "Send thou the children to us that we may place them upon their father's throne."

Clotilde was pleased to do as her sons wished, for she thought she was too old to guard the children well. So, after making a little feast for the princes, she sent them away, never dreaming that any harm could befall them when they were in their uncle's care.

But no sooner had the children reached their uncles than the servants and tutors who had come with them were sent away, while they were shut up in a gloomy room all by themselves.

Then Clotair and Hildebert sent a messenger to Clotilde, bearing in his hands a pair of shears or scissors and a naked sword.

"Most glorious queen," said the messenger when he was shown into her presence, "thy sons and masters desire to know thy will touching these children. Wilt thou that they live with shorn hair or that they be put to death?" You remember that to cut off a prince's long locks was to take from him the sign of his royal birth, when as a rule he entered the Church and became a priest.

Clotilde was so angry and dismayed at this strange message, that scarce knowing what she said, she cried, "If my grandsons are not placed upon their father's throne I would rather see them dead," and the poor queen wrung her hands and wept bitterly.

But the messenger hastened away, and although he knew that Clotilde had not really meant what she said, he told his master that the queen was pleased that the children should be put to death.

Clotair and Hildebert, the two cruel uncles, then sent for the little princes. The eldest, who was only ten years old, began to cry bitterly when he saw that his uncle Clotair held a hunting knife in his hand, but his voice was speedily silenced.

Then the second little prince, who was only seven years old, clung to his uncle Hildebert, begging that he might not be slain as his brother had been. For a moment it seemed as though Hildebert would try to save his little nephew.

But Clotair cried, "Thrust the child from thee, or thou diest in his stead." And Hildebert was afraid, and tried no more to shield his little nephew. Then he too was speedily put to death.

Amid the crowd of cruel men who looked on at Clotair's cruel deeds, one was struck with pity for the little prince who was left. He suddenly caught the child up in his arms and fled with him into the country.

When he was a few years older the prince was taken to church, where his locks were shorn, and in after-days he became a saint. When he became a saint he was named St. Cloud. To-day, close to Paris, on the banks of the Seine, there is a town called St. Cloud, after this little prince who became a saint.

Queen Clotilde wept bitterly when she heard of the

death of her two grandsons, and never did she forgive herself for the hasty words she had spoken.

But Clotair and Hildebert divided their nephews' kingdom, and paid no heed to their mother's tears.

Clovis, you remember, ruled as a king over the Franks, but Clotair was ruled by his warriors, for, many years after the death of the little princes, he refused to lead his people to battle, wishing rather to make peace with the Saxons, a German tribe which had come from the mouth of the Elbe, and was harrying the land.

But the Franks would have nothing to do with so cowardly a king, for such, in truth, they deemed him. They set a guard upon Clotair, tore his tent into pieces, and hurled scorn upon his fears. Then they carried him to the head of his army, saying that if he would not march upon the enemy they would kill him. So Clotair was forced to give battle. But the Saxons fought as men fight for home and country, slaying their foes in great numbers, until even the fierce Franks were themselves glad to sue for peace.

In 558 A.D. Hildebert died, and Clotair then ruled over all the Franks. From this time until his death in 561 he was engaged in wars with different tribes. At last he was stricken with fever, and as he tossed upon his couch he cried, "O how great must be the King of Heaven, if He can thus kill so mighty a king as I."

After Clotair's death the kingdom of the Franks was again divided into four parts. The kings who ruled during the next fifty years committed so many cruel deeds and did so little for their country, that there is nothing to tell you about them in this story. But during these years two queens lived, whose wicked lives have made their names well known in history.

Brunhilda and Fredegonda had each married a grandchild of King Clovis. From the first they hated and were jealous of one another.

THE THREE LITTLE PRINCES 27

When by chance Brunhilda fell into Fredegonda's power, the jealous queen sent her rival Brunhilda to prison, from which, however, she was rescued by a man who loved her. In vain did Fredegonda try again to capture her prisoner. Brunhilda had escaped beyond the reach of the angry queen.

In 584 A.D. it is said that Fredegonda murdered her husband. Many other crimes she certainly committed, but at length in 597 A.D. she died, leaving her son, Clotair II, to rule over part of the Frankish kingdom.

Brunhilda lived still for many years, and during these later years she grew more and more powerful. She also did much good, building churches, and giving alms to the poor. There were many of these who mourned for her after her death.

When she was eighty years of age, Brunhilda fell into the hands of Fredegonda's son, Clotair II., who was now king of all the Franks. Clotair was Brunhilda's enemy, for the old queen had been hated by his mother, and had also, when she was powerful, wrested many provinces from his kingdom. In 613 A.D. he ordered Brunhilda, whose age alone might have aroused his compassion, to be tied to the tail of a wild horse. In this cruel way the poor old queen was trampled to death.

In 628 A.D. Clotair II. died, and Dagobert, his son, at once seized the throne. The times were rough, yet the new king ruled so wisely that he was loved and obeyed by his people.

As he journeyed through his kingdom, he would stop at the towns and villages, that the people might come to tell him their troubles. And because the king was just, and punished the rich if they disobeyed his laws as well as the poor, the nobles did not dare to oppress their vassals so much as they had been used to do.

The king encouraged his people, too, to build churches and to adorn them with the work of skillful goldsmiths.

Because of his justice and his kindness the fame of Dagobert spread all over the land. While he lived his people called him "Great King Dagobert," and for many years after his death his name was remembered with reverence.

CHAPTER VI

THE SLUGGARD KINGS

CLOVIS, you will remember, was the first of the Merovingian monarchs. Dagobert was the last who was worthy to bear the name of king.

After the death of Dagobert twelve princes of his race ruled, but little is remembered of them save only their names.

They were weak and lazy, these Merovingian kings; indeed, they became so lazy that they were called the "Sluggard Kings," and sluggard is a name which no one, and least of all a king, should ever bear.

These sluggard or do-nothing kings sat upon the throne and pretended to rule.

If an ambassador from a distant land came to the court of France, he was brought into the king's presence to deliver his message. And the do-nothing king would seem to listen, but when he answered, the words he spoke were those that had been put into his mouth by his chief minister.

The chief minister of these Merovingian kings was called the Mayor of the Palace. At first these mayors were only stewards of high rank, but when they saw the weakness and laziness of the kings, then, little by little, they seized upon the power which was slipping from the hands of the listless race of Meroveus, and became the real rulers of the land.

You will be almost sorry for these kings, in spite of their foolish lazy ways, when you hear how they were treated by the Mayors of the Palace.

To begin with, the kings had no money, save a small

sum which was given to them by the mayor, and even the amount of that varied according to the minister's mood.

The kings owned no palaces, but were lodged in poorly furnished houses in the country, and there they held their dreary court, surrounded by a few roughly dressed servants.

When they wished to drive, no carriage was ordered for these make-believe kings. A cart drawn by a poke of oxen and guided by a cowherd was the only chariot they knew.

One of the most powerful of the mayors was named Pepin. Pepin was a duke, and although he never tried to change his title to king, he could easily have done so had he wished.

For twenty-seven years Duke Pepin ruled France. While a lazy, shadowy figure sat upon the throne and was called king, Pepin led the warriors forth to battle. And when the Pope, as the Bishop of Rome was now called, sent teachers or missionaries into France, it was Pepin who protected them from the fierce German tribes who were still wandering over the country.

As Christmastide drew near in the year 714 A.D. Pepin died. His son Charles now became Mayor of the Palace.

Charles seemed to think that the Franks could not be ruled unless a king was on the throne. He therefore saw to it that one of the sluggard kings should still sit there, for well he knew that such a king would not interfere with him.

A strong ruler was needed in France, for the country was threatened with a great danger. The Saracens or Arabs, followers of the Prophet Mahomet and enemies of the Cross, had spread all over the southern world.

In India they had taught their faith and put to death those who refused to accept it. In Spain, too, they had forced their faith upon the people, and in 718 A.D. possessed most of that country.

Then in 732 A.D. the Saracens determined to cross the

Pyrenees, the mountains that separated Spain from France. This was the great danger that threatened the country. And you will remember that Charles, in fighting against the Saracens, was fighting for the Christian faith as well as in defense of his country.

The Saracens, having crossed the Pyrenees, fell upon the town of Bordeaux and sacked it. They then crossed the river Garonne, and laid waste the province of Aquitaine.

The leader of the Saracens was named Abdel-Rahman. He had heard of the rich abbeys, filled with treasures, that were to be found in the city of Tours, and thither he now led his army. Already the Saracens were beneath the walls of the city, when they heard that the Franks were approaching in great numbers.

Abdel-Rahman ordered his troops to fall back on Poitiers, a town quite near to Tours, and there, for a week, the two armies faced one another. Then Abdel-Rahman's patience gave way, and at the head of his horsemen he ordered a general attack.

The Franks were already drawn up in battle array. "They stood there," says an old writer, "like solid walls or icebergs, and the Saracens were amazed to see how tall and strong the enemy seemed."

As the battle raged, a small body of Franks crept round to the Arabs' camp, perhaps in the hope of robbing it, or, it may be, wishing to attack the enemy in the rear.

The Saracens had much booty in their camp, and Abdel-Rahman's horsemen seeing the Franks, as they believed, falling upon it, at once left their post to defend their treasure. But they fell into disorder, broke their ranks, and soon the whole army was in confusion. Meanwhile the main body of the Franks, shouting their war-cry, clashing their shields, pressed in among them and beat them down, slaying Abdel-Rahman, their leader.

Night fell, and both armies withdrew to their tents. The Franks were early astir, eager to finish the fight. But in the camp of the Saracens all was strangely still. A few Franks were sent to find out what the enemy was about. They entered the camp unhindered. In the tents not a soldier was to be seen, for under cover of the darkness the Saracens had beat a retreat, leaving their booty behind them.

The battle of Tours or Poitiers, for it is called by either name, was a very important battle, for by the victory of the Franks, not only France, but Europe was saved from becoming the home of the fierce followers of Mahomet the Prophet.

It was because of the heavy blows that Duke Charles showered upon the Saracens at the battle of Tours, that he was from henceforth called Charles Martel, or, as the word Martel means hammer, Charles the Hammer. After the battle of Poitiers in 731 A.D., Charles did not rest until he had swept the Saracens utterly out of France.

To reward his warriors for their valor on the battlefield, Charles the Hammer robbed the churches of their treasures; he even made some of his soldiers bishops and priests. This made the Pope very angry. But it was in vain that he rebuked Charles. Charles was all-powerful and would have his own way.

The Pope's anger did not make the duke cease to protect the missionaries who were sent from Rome to teach the German tribes the faith of Christ.

One of these missionaries was St. Boniface. You will remember his name with interest when I tell you that he was born in Wessex, which was once the name of the southwest of England.

Charles wrote a letter and sent it, not only to the bishops, but to all those dukes and counts who had power in the land, to tell them that St. Boniface was under his care.

St. Boniface was grateful for Charles's protection, and from the heart of Germany, where he was working among

THE SLUGGARD KINGS

the fierce pagan people, he wrote a grateful tribute to the powerful duke.

"Without the patronage of the Prince of the Franks," said St. Boniface, "without his order and the fear of his power, I could not guide this people, or defend the priests . . . and handmaids of God, or forbid in this country the rites of the pagans and their worship of idols."

In 737 A.D. the Merovingian king whom Charles had placed upon the throne died, and during the last few years of his life Charles the Hammer ruled without a shadowy sluggard king sitting upon the throne.

Charles himself died at the age of fifty-two, and his brave warriors wept because he would lead them forth to battle no more.

CHAPTER VII

THE DEATH OF ST. BONIFACE

Before he died, Charles the Hammer divided the kingdom between his two sons, Pepin and Carloman.

Charles had trained his sons to love their country better than themselves, and they worked together for the good of their people, undisturbed by a single jealous thought.

But at the end of six years Carloman grew tired of his share of the task. Knowing that Pepin was able to rule alone, he had his royal locks shorn and entered a monastery, where he was heard of no more.

Pepin was a little man, so his people called him Pepin the Short. But though he was little he had the great gift of courage, and in spite of his small body he was unusually strong.

It is said that soon after his father's death he gave proof of his great strength. The Franks were one day gathered in great numbers round an arena or open space, to watch a cruel combat between two savage beasts. It was their chief amusement to watch such sport, and Duke Pepin was among the spectators.

A lion had just sprung upon a bull and brought it to the ground, when Pepin rose to his feet, and, pointing to the beasts, cried aloud to the Franks, "Which of you will dare to separate them?"

No one answered the terrible challenge. Then Pepin himself sprang into the arena, and fought both the lion and the bull.

THE DEATH OF ST. BONIFACE

The Franks looked on in horror, expecting every moment that Pepin would be torn to pieces. But he overpowered both the savage beasts, and then, tossing away his sword, he cried, "Am I worthy to be your king?" And the rough warriors, to whom kingship meant little save such bravery and strength as Pepin had just shown, shouted aloud that he was worthy.

For ten years Pepin the Short ruled as Mayor of the Palace, the last of the sluggard kings still sitting on the throne where Pepin himself had placed him after the death of Charles the Hammer.

But at the end of ten years Pepin began to think that there was no reason why he should not be king in name as well as in deed.

So he sent to the Pope, who in those days had power over kings, to ask if he, Pepin, might be crowned.

"It is right that the kingly title should rest where the kingly power now is," answered the Pope; and as there was no doubt that Pepin had the "kingly power," the question was settled.

The sluggard king was therefore deposed, his long hair cut off, and he himself shut up in a monastery. And thus ended the race of the Merovingian kings.

Pepin, the new king, was then anointed by St. Boniface, in the presence of his clergy and warriors, with holy oil, which was believed to have come straight from heaven. With Pepin began a new race of kings, called after its founder, Charles the Hammer, the Carlovingian line.

Two years after this Pepin was again anointed with holy oil by the Pope himself, and along with him were consecrated his two sons. One of these sons became the famous Emperor Charlemagne or Charles the Great.

You remember that Charles the Hammer had taken St. Boniface under his protection. Pepin the Short continued to care for the good man, but his power could not save the missionary from a martyr's death.

But before I tell you of the fate which befell the saint, listen to this beautiful story about the holy man.

Once upon a time, in his journeys, the saint came to a land where the rude Northmen still worshiped a god called Thor the Hammerer.

It was winter, and on a little hill a great crowd of warriors clad in white, of women and children, gathered around a fire that had been lighted near the foot of an altar.

Close to the altar was a tall and ancient oak tree, sacred to the god named Thor.

In the midst of the crowd stood the high priest, and at his feet knelt a little child. The little child was the offering of the people to their god. He was doomed to die by a hammer-stroke, that Thor the Hammerer might be pleased.

But ere the hammer fell this wintry night, a quick step came hurrying up the little hill, and Boniface the saint, pushing the people on one side, reached the high priest and the little kneeling child.

Very simply the stranger told the people the story of Jesus and the Cross, and before the tale was ended the hammer had fallen from the hand of the high priest, had fallen harmless to the ground. The little child was saved.

Then seizing the hammer, St. Boniface himself felled the sacred oak, and even as he did so, his eyes fell upon a young fir tree, standing straight and green before him.

"Here is the living tree," he cried, "with no stain of blood upon it, which shall be the sign of your new worship. See, it is pointing to the sky! Let us call it the tree of the Christ Child. Take it up and carry it to the hall of your chief, for this is the birth-night of the White Christ. You shall no more keep your feasts in the shades of the forest with secret and cruel rites. You shall keep them in your own homes, with happy laughter and glad songs of glee."

Such, says the legend, was the beginning of the Christmas tree, which boys and girls all over the world have learned to love.

THE DEATH OF ST BONIFACE

Boniface had been made an archbishop, and had he wished, he might have lived at ease in his palace for the rest of his life. But though he was an old man now, Boniface longed to carry his Master's message to the fierce German tribes which had never even heard of Christ.

So making one of his disciples archbishop in his stead, the old man said, "As for me, I will put myself on my road, for the time of my passing away approacheth. I have longed for this departure and none can turn me from it." It almost seemed that Boniface foresaw what might happen. With only a few followers he set out to find the people whom he wished to teach. When at length he reached their haunts he halted, and his servants put up their master's tent. Then in that wild and lonely place he sat down with his followers to the sacrament of the Lord's Supper.

But a band of savages had seen the white tent, and in their foolish rage they rushed upon the little company. The saint's servants were brave men, and placing their master in their midst, they prepared to defend him unto death.

"Hold, hold!" cried the old man, as he saw them draw their swords; "we should return good for evil, and trust in God"; and then he bade them put their swords back in their sheaths, and strike no blow at the savages whom they had come to teach.

But the barbarians, undaunted by the gentleness of the old man, slew him and as many of his followers as they could seize. Thus perished the holy man of God, St. Boniface.

King Pepin's great work was to help the Pope against the King of the Lombards. To do this he crossed the Alps with his army and marched into Italy.

After a great battle, in which he was victorious, Pepin shut up the King of Lombardy and the soldiers that had been taken prisoners, in a town called Pavia, and made the king promise to stay within the gates of the city. Then with much booty Pepin set off on his homeward march.

But the Pope was not satisfied. He was sure that his enemy would break his word and escape from Pavia, and he wished Pepin had stayed in Italy instead of hastening back to France.

And, indeed, no sooner was Pepin out of the country than the Lombards, more fierce than ever after their defeat, escaped from Pavia, laid waste the country, and began to thunder at the very gates of Rome.

Then a strange thought came to the Pope. It was certain that Pepin would not come back again even at the Pope's request, but if the King of France received a letter from the Apostle Peter, promising to reward him if he helped the Pope, why then without doubt Pepin would come back to Italy.

So the Pope sat down, and while the Lombards thundered at his gates, he wrote a letter from "Peter, Apostle of Jesus Christ," to Pepin and his warriors, to tell them that "if they came in haste to help the Pope, he, Peter, would aid them as if he were alive, and that they would conquer their enemies as well as win eternal life."

As the Pope had foreseen when he wrote that strange letter, Pepin, when he read it, did not hesitate to return to Italy. Once again he crossed the Alps, and once again he conquered the Lombards and shut them up in Pavia, and this time, anxious for peace at any price, the King of Lombardy kept the terms imposed upon him by Pepin.

When the battle was over, Pepin sent for the keys of the towns which he had taken from the Lombards, and these he sent to Rome to be laid on the altar of the church of St. Peter. In reality, to give the keys to St. Peter's was to give the towns to which they belonged to the Pope.

This gift was known as the "Donation of Pepin." It was no strange thing for kings in those days to offer their victories to God. But you will remember Pepin's gift to

St. Peter's because it was the beginning of the worldly possessions of the popes.

Soon after this, as King Pepin was returning home from battle, he was attacked by fever. His servants carried him to St. Denis, where he died, having ruled France for sixteen years.

CHAPTER VIII

ROLAND WINDS HIS HORN

Before his death Pepin had divided his kingdom between his two sons, but in three years Carloman died. Charles, soon to be called Charlemagne or Charles the Great, ruled alone as King of the Franks.

As his father had done, so Charlemagne also marched into Italy with his brave warriors and punished the Lombards, who had again dared to besiege the city of Rome.

At home, too, the king had little peace, for again and again the Saxons invaded his land. The great king conquered them, and for a time they would live quietly and be obedient to their conqueror. But as soon as he went away to fight in distant lands they rebelled, and for thirty years Charlemagne waged war against them.

When Charlemagne had conquered one of these tribes, he would offer to pardon them if they would give up their false gods and be baptized. If they refused to be baptized, their heads were cut off.

As you can imagine, many Saxon tribes were willing to be baptized rather than to suffer death. After their baptism, Charlemagne would send missionaries to the people, and thus little by little the teaching of the White Christ became better known.

Around the name of this great King Charles, as around the name of our own King Arthur, have gathered many legends or marvelous tales. These tales may not all be true, for legends are woven out of fancy as well as fact. But sometimes legends help us to understand a man or

ROLAND WINDS HIS HORN

woman, a country or an age, better than we should if fancy had been idle and left facts untouched.

And so, although part of the story of the battle of Roncesvalles, in which Roland, Charlemagne's nephew, fought so bravely, is not told to us in history but only in legend, yet it is none the less worthy to be read.

The great battle of which I wish to tell you took place in the valley of Roncesvalles.

Spain, as you have already heard, had been conquered by the Saracens, those fierce followers of the Prophet Mahomet. But they began to quarrel and fight among themselves, and at last their King, Marsil, begged Charlemagne to come and help him against his own rebellious people, who were trying to wrest from him the beautiful city of Saragossa.

Charlemagne did not need to be asked twice. To him it was enough that those he was asked to fight were infidels, followers of Mahomet and not of Christ. He would destroy these fierce Saracens, or baptize them as he had baptized the pagan Saxons at home.

So, to the joy of the King of Saragossa, Charlemagne set out for Spain at the head of his brave Frankish warriors.

To reach Saragossa the king had to lead his army through the valley of Roncesvalles. The valley was really a narrow pass through which the army could march only in a long thin line. Should an enemy steal down the mountains and fall upon the soldiers as they struggled along the narrow pass, nothing could save them. But no foe was in ambush, and the great army passed in safety out of the valley of Roncesvalles.

But when Charlemagne had laid siege to Saragossa his difficulties began, for at once the Saracens stopped fighting among themselves, to fight together against the foe who had besieged their city. Marsil, too, proved false, for he slew the ambassadors of the French king, although he had sent them the olive branch of peace. He had indeed no need of Charlemagne now that the Saracens had ceased to fight against him, and would gladly have seen Charlemagne and his army return to their own land.

Meanwhile in the French camp provisions ran short and sickness broke out among the soldiers. Tidings also came from France telling of new invasions by the Saxons. So when Marsil sent to beseech Charlemagne to raise the siege and make peace with him, the king was more pleased than the Saracens knew.

Now in history we hear little of Charlemagne's return to France. But in a poem called "The Song of Roland," which was loved by the Franks and often sung by them as they marched to battle, the sad tale has been told. And if the story of the treachery of King Marsil and all that befell Roland and his friend Oliver in the valley of Roncesvalles is partly legend, it is, as I have told you, not the less worthy to be heard.

King Marsil had promised that if Charlemagne would go back to his fair realm of France, he would become his vassal and be baptized in the name of the Holy Christ.

Charlemagne did not know if he could trust the heathen lord, so he called together a council of war, and told his barons and knights King Marsil's words. "Yet whether he spoke the truth or falsehood I know not," said Charlemagne.

Then up sprang Roland, Charlemagne's own nephew, and the bravest knight of France, crying, "Trust not this traitor Marsil. He sent thee the olive branch of peace, yet he slew thine ambassador. Let us fight, nor heed the false words of the traitor king."

As Roland ceased speaking, Ganelon, his stepfather, rose, and an angry scowl was upon his face, for he hated Roland, although others loved him well.

"Heed not the brave words of my stepson Roland," he said. "Accept King Marsil's promises, lest we tarry here and are slain."

Still Charlemagne sat silent, waiting, lest other knights had aught to say.

Then the wisest man in the king's council arose. "The words of Ganelon are full of wisdom," he said. "Let us make peace with King Marsil and return to our own land."

"As thou sayest so shall it be," answered Charlemagne, and he commanded Ganelon to go tell Marsil that Charlemagne would accept his homage and look for him to come to the fair realm of France to be baptized in the name of Christ.

Ganelon was ill-pleased to be sent to the King of Saragossa, lest he should prove false and slay him even as he had already slain other ambassadors. And because he was angry, he vowed to bring shame upon Charlemagne and Roland, whom he hated.

Thus before Ganelon had spoken long with King Marsil he had won for himself rich gifts, but he had betrayed Charlemagne and offered up Roland to death, as you shall hear.

When the ambassador returned to the French camp, he told Charlemagne that he might well trust King Marsil to do all that he had promised.

Charlemagne was filled with foreboding, he knew not why. Yet he ordered the trumpets to sound and the great army to prepare to start on its homeward journey.

But all unknown to the Franks, silent and still, there stole after them, through the forests and along the mountain tops, the hosts of King Marsil. For thus had it been planned by the traitor Ganelon.

As they drew near to the valley of Roncesvalles, Charlemagne ordered his army to halt. His distrust of King Marsil was not allayed. "Were the enemy to prove false," he said to his lords, "it would go ill with us as we march through this pass. Who will guard the entrance to the valley while we march onward?"

"Entrust the rearguard to Roland," said Ganelon quickly, "for who is so brave a knight as he." But in his heart Ganelon laughed, for well he knew that the hosts of Marsil would fall upon Roland and his knights, and slay them before Charlemagne was aware.

The king looked with displeasure at Ganelon. Yet it was foolish to dream that one of his own knights would betray the army. So, as Roland also pleaded that the post of danger might be given to him, Charlemagne yielded at last, saying, "Half of the army shall I leave with thee to guard the pass."

"Nay," said Roland, "twenty thousand men only will I have." And Ganelon, as he heard his stepson's words, was well pleased.

Then the great army passed on, leaving Roland to guard the entrance to the valley of Roncesvalles. With him were his friend Oliver, the bold Archbishop Turpin, the twelve chosen peers of France, and twenty thousand of Charlemagne's bravest knights.

Among the army there were many who would fain have stayed with Roland. But sadder than any of his soldiers was the great king himself. Fear was in his heart, tears in his eyes, for ever his heart whispered to him that Roland was betrayed. Yet, saying farewell to his dauntless rearguard, Charlemagne marched on at the head of his army.

Roland and his knights were now left alone, and the great host of the Saracens was drawing near. Soon Roland could hear the tramp of armed men.

Then Oliver, his friend, climbed out of the valley on to the top of a hill, and lo! he saw a great host approaching, and he knew that Roland was betrayed, and by the false traitor Ganelon.

Down again to the valley ran Oliver and told Roland what he had seen.

"Wind a loud blast upon thy horn," cried Oliver. "Our king will hear and hasten back to our aid." For ever round his neck the knight wore an ivory horn. It had a note of magic, and if Roland blew it in time of need the sound was carried on and ever on. Neither lofty mountains nor dense forests could dull the sweet clear tone of Roland's magic horn.

"Blow thy horn," cried Oliver, but alas, this Roland would not do.

And now with mocking words the heathen host rushed upon the hero and his twenty thousand knights.

"Ye are sold, sold and betrayed by your king," they shouted.

Roland heard the base lie, and furiously he rode against the foe, striking fierce blows with his good sword Durindal.

Listen to the "Song of Roland" as it tells how Roland looked that day:

> "Oh in his harness he looks grand;
> On, on he goes with lance on high,
> Its tip is pointed to the sky;
> It bears a snow-white pennon, and
> Its golden fringes sweep his hand."

Oliver and the brave Archbishop Turpin fought as they had never fought before, as did also the knights, until King Marsil's host lay slain upon the ground.

Four hundred thousand strong had been the heathen hosts, and but one was left to tell King Marsil the dread tidings that his army had perished.

When Marsil heard that Roland was still alive and that all his hosts were slain, his rage was terrible.

Without a moment's delay he assembled another great army, and himself marched at its head toward the valley of Roncesvalles.

As he drew near to the battlefield, he divided his army. Sending one division to fight the Franks, he kept the other back on the hillside to watch how the battle went.

Then, when Roland saw another force approaching, he rallied his knights to a fresh attack, and so valiantly did they fight, that erelong the heathen host fled, calling upon Marsil for help.

There were now but three hundred of Charlemagne's peerless warriors on the battlefield. The others were dead or wounded. But the handful of gallant knights never flinched as King Marsil himself advanced upon them with his men. And ever in the forefront of the battle rode Roland, and by his side was Oliver.

At length, when but sixty Franks were left, Archbishop Turpin besought Roland to sound his horn, that Charlemagne might hear and come back to avenge the death of so many of his peerless knights.

Then Roland, thinking it now no shame to wind his horn, did as the good archbishop wished. And far away a note, clear but faint, fell upon the ear of Charlemagne.

"It is the ivory horn I hear," he cried. "Roland hath need of us."

But Ganelon was by the king's side, and he laughed, saying, "It is but the wind that my lord hears, as it whistles among the trees."

So Charlemagne, for all that he was ill at ease, rode on.

Once again Roland placed the horn to his lips, but he was faint from many wounds, and the note he blew was sad and low. Yet on and on it journeyed, until far away the great king heard the mournful sound.

"Roland hath need of us," he cried, as the sound crept into his heart. "There hath surely been a battle." Yet, for Ganelon still mocked at the king's fears, Charlemagne moved on toward France, but now he rode more slowly.

Once more Roland blew his ivory horn, but he was weak from loss of blood, and it was a sad sweet note that reached the king.

Charlemagne's knights heard the note also, and cried, "It is Roland who calls us, for his need is great. He has been betrayed," and they looked darkly at the traitor Ganelon.

ROLAND WINDS HIS HORN

Then Charlemagne hesitated no longer. He ordered his army to turn and march back to the valley of Roncesvalles. And because the soldiers loved Roland well, each one put spurs to his horse and rode in haste to his comrade's aid.

As for Ganelon, the king gave him into the charge of the kitchen knaves, who beat him and called him traitor and false knight.

For it was indeed Ganelon who had said to Marsil, "If you kill Roland, there will be no one left to be your enemy. For Charlemagne grows old, and there is no knight so bold as Roland." He had promised that Roland and no other should be left at Roncesvalles, and that but a few knights should stay with him. And for this treachery he had received rich gifts from King Marsil. Well might the kitchen knaves call Ganelon traitor and false knight.

On the battlefield at Roncesvalles there were now left alive only Roland, the brave priest Turpin, and a noble count. Oliver had perished with the other knights.

The heathen host was still more than a thousand strong, yet so bravely did the three warriors stand that they dared not attack them. Only from afar they hurled their javelins at the dauntless three, until, pierced by a dart, the count fell dead.

Roland too was sore wounded, but yet again he blew his ivory horn. Faint and dull the notes were wafted on the breeze, faint and dull they fell upon the ear of Charlemagne.

"Let my trumpets sound," cried the king, "that Roland may know we come. Sore wounded must he be, or not thus would he wind his horn."

Then loud sounded the trumpets of the Franks, and the heathen host heard the blast, and knowing that the great king was coming to avenge the death of his knights, they fled, hurling their spears at the two heroes who alone were left on the battlefield.

One of the spears struck the good archbishop, and he fell to the ground. Roland only was left alive.

But he too was nigh to death. With one last effort he placed his good sword Durindal and his ivory horn beneath his body, that there Charlemagne might find them when he came.

> "Then not unmindful of His care,
> Once more he sues to God for grace.
> 'O Thou true Father of us all . . .
> From all the perils I deserve
> For sinful life, my soul preserve.'
>
> "Then to his God out stretcheth he
> The glove from his right hand—and see!
> St. Gabriel taketh it instantly.
> God sends a cherub—angel bright,
> And Michael, Saint of Peril hight—
> And Gabriel comes; up, up they rise,
> And bear the Count to Paradise."

God had Roland's soul safe in Paradise, but his body lay quiet and still on the battlefield, and there Charlemagne found it, with the sword and magic horn beneath.

Sorely did the great king grieve for Roland and his peerless knights, yet did he not tarry on the battlefield to weep. But at the head of his army he followed the heathen host, nor did he order the trumpets to sound the retreat until every one of the vast army was slain.

Ganelon, the traitor, suffered a terrible death, for by the order of Charlemagne and the judgment of the knights of France, he was torn to pieces by wild horses.

During his long reign Charlemagne had often helped the Pope against his enemies.

When Leo III. became Pope, he was glad to have the great king as his friend, and in 799 A.D., when the Romans rebelled against him, Leo fled to Charlemagne for help.

The king agreed to punish the Pope's enemies, and send him back in safety to Rome. Perhaps it was in gratitude

ROLAND WINDS HIS HORN

that Leo III. then agreed to crown Charlemagne Emperor of the West.

You remember that Romulus, the last emperor, had been deposed in 476 A.D., and since then there had been no Emperor of the West.

But now, on Christmas Day, in the year 800 A.D., Charlemagne, who had journeyed to Rome, went into the great church of St. Peter's. As he knelt before the altar the Pope placed a crown upon his head, while all the people who had crowded into the church shouted, "Long life and victory to Charles, Emperor of the Romans!"

It was an empty title, for the Romans had now no power and no position in the world.

But the Pope having bestowed the title upon Charlemagne, he henceforth ruled over his great kingdom as emperor.

All Gaul from the Rhine to the Pyrenees was his; also, for the most part, Italy and all central and western Germany belonged to him, while many races, scattered over the world, owned their allegiance to the Emperor Charlemagne.

For fourteen years there was now peace in France, and during these years the emperor worked as hard as he had done in time of war.

You will be surprised to hear that though he was an old man now, he was so anxious to learn that he studied harder than any schoolboy. Astronomy, arithmetic, grammar, and music, these were some of the studies that were dear to the emperor. But he had never learned to write, and that was Charlemagne's great ambition. So he was often to be seen walking about with tablets in his hand, and at every odd moment he would practice making letters. But he never knew them well enough to do more than sign his name.

The emperor was anxious that the boys and girls in his land should learn the things which he had never been taught when he was young, so he built schools and sent scholars to teach in them. But there were lazy pupils then just as there are lazy pupils now, and when the emperor visited the schools, he would tell the lazy boys and girls how sorry they would be if they grew up, as he had done, without even knowing how to write. And then the boys and girls would do their lessons better, until they forgot the emperor's words, and began to grow lazy once more.

The great emperor was old now, and his long reign was nearly over. He was more than seventy years of age when he grew ill and died.

His people buried him near to his favorite hunting ground. Upon his knees they placed an open Bible, on which rested the little purse filled with alms which he had carried with him to Rome. Upon his head they left his crown, his good sword lying by his side, while at his feet rested his shield and the scepter he had wielded so wisely and so well.

CHAPTER IX

LOUIS THE GOOD-NATURED

THE new king had begun to reign over one of his father's provinces when he was a little child of three years old. At least, if he did not reign, he had really been anointed with holy oil just as a grown-up king would have been.

After he had been anointed, the little boy was carried in his cradle to the entrance of his kingdom. Here his courtiers halted. They did not wish their baby-king to enter his dominions in a cradle. So they clad the little king in a tiny suit of armor and gave him tiny arms, that looked more like toys than weapons. Then these gallant courtiers brought a horse and put his little Highness on its back and held him there, safe and sound and perhaps crowing with delight, until he had entered his royal province amid the cheers of the people.

But that was long ago, when Charlemagne's strong arm could reach to the kingdom of his little son and keep order and peace for him during his boyhood's days. After his father's long reign was ended, it was this same son, grown now to be a man, who ruled over Charlemagne's great empire.

Louis was not strong and wise as his father had been. He was indeed so gentle and so easily pleased, that his people called him Louis the Good-natured.

King Louis had been taught by priests when he was a little boy, and when he grew older he followed their teaching better than they did themselves. He determined that when he was king, the priests should live more simply than they had done in his father's time.

The priests had arms, for in those days they were to be seen on the battlefield as well as in the church. But King Louis bade them lay down their arms. They must not fight with swords and spears as other men, but with gentleness and kindly words and deeds.

The priests had horses, for in those days they rode on as noble war-steeds as did the bravest knights. But King Louis bade them put away their horses. It was not meet for them to ride on noble steeds, for their Master was lowly and had ridden on an ass.

Many of the monks were greedy and selfish, and had used their power to wring money from the people. Louis cared for the poor and forbade the monks to oppress them.

You can imagine, then, that King Louis was no favorite with the bishops and priests, but if they were displeased, the people were loud in their praise of Louis the Good-natured.

Now King Louis had four sons, and as they grew up they were quick to take advantage of their father's good-nature. Again and again they rebelled against him. At last even Louis was roused, and took away from Pippin, the most troublesome of his sons, the province over which he ruled, and gave it to his youngest son, Charles the Bald.

The three eldest sons then assembled an army to fight against their father. The king also gathered his soldiers together, but when the two armies met on a field called the Field of Red, many of King Louis's soldiers left him and joined themselves to the rebels. For this reason the battle-field was ever after called "The Field of Falsehood."

Louis, when he saw that he was left with only a few followers, bade them also go away, for he was unwilling that any one should "lose life or limb" for his sake. Then he surrendered himself to his sons, who treated him very badly, for they forced him to confess in church, before his people, a long list of crimes which he had never committed.

King Louis's good-nature had turned into weakness, and he obediently read aloud the list of crimes of which he was guiltless. Then, laying aside his royal robes, he allowed himself to be clad in sackcloth, and walked barefooted through the streets of the city, no longer a king but a prisoner.

But now that they had got their father out of the way, the four sons quarreled so fiercely among themselves, that their subjects grew discontented, and began to wish that Louis the Good-natured was still upon the throne. And at length they actually revolted, and set Louis free and made him king once more.

You would expect Louis to punish his sons for their bad behavior, but he never seemed to dream of such a thing. So, when the chance came, they again took up arms against their father. King Louis was ill and worn out with the troubles of his reign, yet he went at the head of his army to put down the rebellion, and this time his sons were forced to submit to him.

But the effort had been too much for the king. He took fever and died on a little island in the river Rhine.

His last words were words of forgiveness to the son who was named after him. "I forgive my son," he said, "but let him remember that he has brought his father's gray hairs in sorrow to the grave."

CHAPTER X

THE VIKINGS

CHARLES the Bald began to reign in 843 A.D. At first his eldest brother laid plots against him, as he had done against their father, to take his kingdom away.

But Charles the Bald made friends with his brother Louis, and together they fought at Fontanet in 841 A.D. against their cruel and ambitious eldest brother.

It was a terrible battle, lasting from dawn until midday, when Charles and Louis were victorious. But so many soldiers had been slain that all over France there were sad and empty homes.

"Accursed be this day," wrote one of the officers who fought at the battle of Fontanet:

> "Be it unlit by the light of the sun,
> Be it without either dawn or twilight . . .
> Eye ne'er hath seen more fearful slaughter . . .
> The linen vestments of the dead did whiten the field
> Even as it is whitened by the birds of Autumn."

Two years after the battle of Fontanet the brothers agreed to fight no more, but to divide the great kingdom between them. Accordingly, at the Treaty of Verdun in 843 A.D., Charles received the kingdom of France, Louis Germany, while to Lothair was given Italy and the name of Emperor.

After this battle Charles the Bald was really King of France, but he had not much power except in the city of Paris; for the lords and barons were kings on their own lands, and were used to make their own laws and impose

THE VIKINGS

taxes on their people. Indeed, there was no limit to their power.

The king gave lands and castles to the barons on what was called the feudal system.

The feudal system meant that the barons became vassals to the king. They were bound to do homage to him for their lands and to fight for him in time of war.

In the same way the barons gave portions of their land to the people who became their vassals, and in time of war had to follow their lord to the battlefield, even as the lords followed the king.

When they were not fighting, the barons were hunting or feasting. They never dreamed of working, that was fit only for the serfs or slaves, who were bought or sold with the land as though they were tools.

These slaves were badly clothed and badly fed. Often, when the harvest was poor, they were starved. Yet the barons still feasted in their halls, heedless of the hunger and misery of the people who were huddled together in the huts that stood at their very doors.

After Charles the Bald had conquered his eldest brother at the battle of Fontanet, his greatest troubles were caused by the Vikings or Northmen.

Even in the time of Charlemagne these wild sea-rovers had reached the coast of France, only however to set their sails, and disappear as suddenly as they had come, when they heard that the great emperor was near. For Charlemagne was the only name the Northmen feared.

Charlemagne himself had foreseen what would happen when he was no longer alive to guard his kingdom from these fierce Vikings.

As he sat at dinner one day in a seaport town, the emperor saw vessels at anchor in the harbor.

"These are trading vessels," cried his lords, "from Africa, from Britain, or elsewhere."

"Nay," answered Charlemagne, "these vessels be not laden with merchandise, but manned with cruel foes."

Then getting up from the table, he went to the window and watched the red sails of the Northmen's ships as they took to flight.

Tears fell from the emperor's eyes as he turned to his followers. "Know ye, my lieges, why I weep so bitterly," he asked. "Of a surety, I fear not lest these fellows should succeed in injuring me by their miserable piracies; but it grieveth me deeply that whilst I live they should have been nigh enough to touch at this shore. I am a prey to violent sorrow when I foresee what evils they will heap upon my descendants and their people."

In the reign of Louis the Good-natured, what Charlemagne had foreseen came to pass.

The terrible Northmen from Norway, Denmark, and Sweden descended upon the coast of France, and laid waste all the towns and villages to which they came. In the time of Charles the Bald the red sails of the Viking ships were known and feared not only in France, but all over Europe.

More than once, in this reign, the Vikings reached Paris, and the citizens, fearing lest their homes and churches should be plundered and destroyed, offered the Northmen large sums of money if they would but sail away and leave their homes and sanctuaries unharmed.

This, as you can easily believe, made the Vikings return again and again, in the hope of being paid a heavy ransom to depart.

These fierce sea-rovers had no respect for church or priest.

Hasting was the name of one of the chief leaders of the Northmen. Wonderful tales were told of this man, of his cruelty and his craft, so that when he actually landed on the coast of France the people were full of fear.

THE VIKINGS

This is one of the stories that the French folk had heard of Hasting.

It was not often that this chief found a town too strongly guarded to be taken by his rough followers. But once upon a time, finding he could not take a certain city by assault, he determined to enter it by craft, or, as you would say, by a trick.

He sent to the bishop of the town, saying that he was very ill and wished to be baptized in the name of the Holy Christ.

The bishop, pleased with such a wish from a Viking chief, hastened to baptize Hasting as he desired.

Soon after this his comrades spread the tidings that their chief was dead. They then went to the bishop, and begged that he might be buried as a Christian, and have a solemn service held over his coffin.

To this also the bishop willingly agreed, and the coffin of the great Viking was carried into church, followed closely by a band of Northmen.

Picture the good bishop's dismay when, in the middle of the service, Hasting, strong and fierce as ever, suddenly leaped from his coffin, sword in hand. His followers at once drew their swords from beneath their cloaks and closed the church doors.

Then the kind bishop and all the priests who were present at the service were slain. The band of robbers seized the rich treasures of the sanctuary, and escaped to their ships and sailed away before the horrified citizens, who had also come to the burial service of the Viking chief, had found time or courage to stop them.

After hearing such a tale, it was little wonder that the French dreaded this Viking chief.

When Hasting arrived at Paris, Charles the Bald sent the Abbot of St. Denis, "the which was an exceeding wise man," to talk with the Viking. This worthy abbot, after promising Hasting large sums of money, actually succeeded in persuading him to give up his roving life and to become a Christian.

Charles the Bald thereupon made him a count, and gave him gifts of land and castles, and for many years the Viking chief kept faith with the kings of France.

Soon after this Charles the Bald was in Italy, and as he was crossing the Alps on his way home he was taken ill. His servants could find no shelter on the mountains for the king, save in a comfortless hut, and there Charles the Bald died, at the age of fifty-four.

His son Louis the Stammerer, who succeeded him, was a delicate prince who reigned only about a year. He was followed by his brother Carloman, of whom there is nothing to tell, save that after reigning for two years he was gored to death by a boar as he was hunting in the royal forests.

CHAPTER XI

THE VIKINGS BESIEGE PARIS

THE names given by the French to their kings in these olden days were sometimes strangely undignified, as you will agree when I tell you that the next king to reign was Charles the Fat.

Charles was indeed of an enormous size, and unfortunately he was as lazy as he was fat.

The story of the reign of Charles the Fat is really the story of how the Northmen besieged Paris, while the king, who was also Emperor of Germany, spent his time among his German barons.

Rollo was the name of the chief who now led the Vikings to Paris. He was a greater chief even than Hasting, of whom you read in the last chapter.

Seven hundred huge ships, with bright red sails, were one day seen to be making their way up the river Seine. These ships were the Viking fleet under Rollo.

The people of Paris resolved to defend their city against the fierce Northmen as long as they could.

Soon they heard that the town of Rouen, which is only a short distance from Paris, had been taken, and that Rollo with thirty thousand men was marching on Paris.

Hasting, now a respectable count, was sent to ask Rollo what he wished.

"Valiant warrior," said Hasting to Rollo, "whence come ye? What seek ye here? What is the name of your lord and master? Tell us this, for we be sent unto you by the King of the Franks."

"We be Danes," answered Rollo, "and all be equally masters among us. We be come to drive out the inhabitants of this land, and subject it to our country. But who art thou who speakest so glibly?"

Then, perhaps with some shame in his face, Hasting told how he had once been, as Rollo now was, a Viking chief. But Rollo interrupted him, saying with scorn, "We have heard tell of that fellow. Hasting began well and ended ill."

But the former chief had no wish to be taunted by Rollo. It may be the sight of the wild sea-robbers had brought to life a hidden wish to be again a lawless roving chief. In any case he stopped Rollo's taunts, demanding roughly, "Will ye yield you to the Emperor Charles?"

"We yield," answered Rollo, "to none. All that we take by our arms we will keep as our right. Go and tell this, if thou wilt, to the emperor whose envoy thou boastest to be."

So Hasting, none too pleased, withdrew from his meeting with Rollo, the chief of the Viking band.

It was the dreary month of November, 885 A.D., when Rollo led his army beneath the walls of Paris. But when he saw the great ramparts and defenses of the city, he hesitated to begin the attack.

Instead, he begged to speak with the bishop of the city, and being admitted to his presence he said, "Take pity on thyself and on thy flock. Let us pass through this city, and we will in no wise touch the town."

But the bishop was too wise to trust the Viking's words. Charles the Fat was in Germany, and had left the city in his charge, and in that of a brave man called Count Eudes.

So the bishop answered Rollo, "This city hath been entrusted to us by our king. If the city had been entrusted to thee, wouldst thou do as thou biddest me?"

"Nay," said Rollo, "sooner would I be slain than betray

THE VIKINGS BESIEGE PARIS 61

my trust. Yet if thou yield not we will besiege thee, and famine shall force thee to give us the city."

But the bishop and Count Eudes agreed with the Viking in one thing. Sooner would they too be slain than betray their trust, so there was nothing for Rollo to do but fulfill his threat and besiege the city.

Thirteen months passed slowly away, for Rollo had surrounded Paris, and as each day dragged its slow length, the citizens were ever in sorer straits. Food grew scarce and famine stared the citizens in the face.

Messengers had been sent to Charles the Fat, telling him of the needs of his faithful subjects in Paris, but he was lazy and paid no heed to their distress.

Then Count Eudes determined that he would go to the king to ask him why he delayed to send help to his loyal citizens.

It was no easy matter to get through the enemy's lines, but messengers had already done so, and Count Eudes was brave and, when it was necessary, careful, and he got away unseen by the Northmen.

But by and by it became known that Count Eudes had escaped from the besieged city, and every opening was now strictly guarded by the enemy, that he might not be able to get back into Paris.

The citizens knew that the Vikings were on the watch for their brave leader, and they crowded on to the ramparts and towers watching anxiously for him to appear.

At length the count was seen in the distance. What would he do? Would he forsake the city seeing it so closely guarded?

The people trembled at the thought, for Count Eudes was brave and had won their trust.

But if the count was careful he was also, if need be, rash. As he drew near to the city, he saw that he could enter it only in one way.

Putting spurs to his powerful war-horse, he rode straight

forward through the lines of the bewildered Northmen, striking boldly with his battle-ax all who dared to come in his way. But, indeed, there were few who opposed the count. His boldness had so startled the Vikings, that Count Eudes was safe within the walls of the city before they had recovered from their surprise. As for the citizens, they welcomed the count's return with laughter and tears, as a starving people might well do.

Count Eudes had, however, succeeded in rousing the indolent king; for in November 886 A.D., after Paris had been besieged for a year, Charles the Fat did actually appear before the city with a large army.

But, after all, he proved a coward and a sluggard. In spite of the large army, he had not come to fight. About a month later, to the unspeakable anger of Count Eudes and the citizens, they found that Charles had bribed the Vikings with large sums of money to raise the siege of Paris.

So angry were the people, not only in Paris, but throughout France, that early in the following year they met together and deposed Charles the Fat, because he was not fit to be a king. Soon after Charles the Fat died in a monastery.

CHAPTER XII

ROLLO'S PRIDE

Count Eudes, who had won the hearts of the people during the siege of Paris, now became King of France.

His most troublesome foe was Rollo, the Northman, who not only seized many important towns, but at the same time took pains to win the friendship of the citizens he had conquered.

When Eudes died, ten years later, his brother, Count Robert of Paris, advised the new king to make terms with Rollo.

Charles the Simple was a lad, barely nineteen years of age, and he followed Count Robert's advice, sending ambassadors to Rollo, to offer him lands and the hand of the French princess, if he would become a Christian and a vassal of the king.

Rollo promised to give up his roving ways and become a loyal subject.

So the king gave his new vassal the beautiful country which lay between the river Seine and the sea. And that part of France is now called Normandy, because the Northmen or Normans settled there.

It was the custom for every new vassal to go to the king's palace to take the oath of fealty to the sovereign.

Charles the Simple was surrounded by his courtiers when Rollo arrived. It was also, I should tell you, usual, after the oath was taken, for the vassal to kneel to kiss the king's foot.

But Rollo, though he was willing to take the oath of

allegiance to Charles, was by no means willing to humble himself by kneeling to kiss the foot of the king. Moreover, his wild life had taught him little respect for such foolish customs.

"Never will I bend the knee to any man, nor will I kiss the foot of any man," cried Rollo, in a voice that no one dared to gainsay.

But some one must kiss the king's foot, and if Rollo would not, well, one of the Norman soldiers should do it in his stead.

So a rough Viking was unwillingly pushed to the front. At his master's command, refusing to kneel, he seized the king's foot and thrust it carelessly against his face, causing Charles to fall backward on his seat, amid the rude jests and laughter of the Northmen.

Rollo was now created the first Duke of Normandy, and this wild sea-roving Northman became the great-grandfather of William the Conqueror.

The nobles, with Count Robert of Paris at their head, now began to grow angry with their king, because he would have nothing to do with them, but chose as his favorite a man of humble birth, who was dishonest, and who daily grew more proud and haughty.

At length Count Robert demanded that the favorite should be dismissed, and when the king refused to listen to his demand, all the nobles rebelled and fought a great battle against Charles at Soissons in 923 A.D.

The nobles won the day, but Count Robert was slain. War, however, was still carried on by his son, Hugh the White, until at length Charles was a prisoner in the hands of his barons. For seven years he was carried from dungeon to dungeon, until he died.

Hugh the White, had he wished it, might now have become king, but intsead of ruling himself, he sent for Louis, the son of Charles the Simple, who had been brought up in England.

Louis did little save quarrel with his nobles, as did also his son and grandson when they, each in his turn, became King of France.

And during these reigns the nobles grew ever more powerful, until Hugh the White's son, Hugh Capet, Count of France, was king in all but name.

CHAPTER XIII

KING ROBERT AND THE POPE

The Merovingian race of kings began with Clovis, and ended with a shadowy figure of a king called Chilperic. The Carlovingian race began with Pepin and ended with Louis v.

Hugh Capet, Count of Paris, had been the most powerful noble in France for several years before he became king.

In 987 A.D., however, he was raised to the throne by the nobles of northern France, and thus he became the founder of the Capetian line of kings.

Hugh's name Capet is said by some to have been given to him because, instead of a crown, he always wore a "cape," "cap," or "hood," dedicated to one of the saints called St. Martin. Others tell us that the size of the king's head made his people call him Capet, *caput* being the Latin word for head.

Although the nobles had given Hugh the title of King, they still considered themselves, if not quite, yet almost his equal. They could not forget that but lately he had held only the title of Count.

Some of the lords, especially those in the south of France, who had had nothing to do with bestowing on Hugh the title of King, refused to do homage to him as their sovereign. Others were outwardly loyal, but in their hearts they resented Hugh Capet's claims.

The king took no pains to soothe the pride of these haughty nobles. Indeed, his treatment made them even more resentful of his authority.

KING ROBERT AND THE POPE

"Who made thee a count?" indignantly demanded Hugh of a noble who behaved in his presence as though the sovereign were still only the Count of Paris.

"Who made thee a king?" quickly retorted the count, to which rough answer, as far as we know, the king had nothing to say.

During the nine years that he reigned Hugh was constantly trying to weaken the power of the nobles. As he grew stronger he would punish them, too, for their haughty ways.

But, in spite of all he could do, the nobles remained more powerful than the king wished. To strengthen himself still more against his enemies, Hugh therefore thought it would be well to win the favor of the bishops and priests. He had inherited many rich lands and abbeys from his father, Hugh the White, and these he now bestowed upon the Church. He thus gained the goodwill of the clergy, and when they called him the "Defender of the Church," the title pleased him well. But what perhaps pleased him still more was that the bishops, who were powerful, and had great influence with the people, took his side against the barons.

After Hugh had been made "Defender of the Church," he would often lay aside his royal robes and appear before his people in the dress of an abbot.

His last words to his son Robert, who succeeded him in 996 A.D., were to bid him ever cherish the Church, and protect her treasures.

It was during the reign of Hugh Capet that the difference in language, in dress, and in manners, between the north and the south of France, became clear.

Those who lived in the south laughed at the way the people in the north pronounced their words. It was so much rougher and harsher than their way.

In dress, too, the southern people were more gay, and, as we would say, more fashionable, while their manners were more polished and polite than those of the people who lived in the north of France. But in another chapter you will read more about those who lived in the south.

Robert the Pious began to reign when he was twenty years old. He was a gentle, simple prince, who loved music, and often he was to be seen in the church of St. Denis, singing in the choir, side by side with the monks.

"He read his Psalter daily," says an old chronicler, "and was gentle, gracious, polished, and he sincerely loved to do a kindness."

But these were rough days in which Robert the Pious lived, and his people often misunderstood or even despised his goodness, while of his kindness they were not slow to take advantage.

One day King Robert saw a priest, as he left church, steal a silver candlestick from the altar. Instead of reproving the thief, Robert the Pious said to him, "Friend, run for your life to your home," and at the same time he gave him money for the journey.

Meanwhile the candlestick was missed, and the priests began to search for the thief.

The king said nothing until he thought the man was far away. Then he asked the anxious seekers, "Why trouble yourselves so much about a candlestick? God has given it to one of his poor."

When Robert went for a journey, it was not in royal state, but accompanied only by twelve poor men. One of these poor men, knowing the king's gentleness, dared to cut a rich gold ornament from his robe. The king, though he saw what the poor man was doing, left him unrebuked.

The rough barons of France had little sympathy with Robert's ways, and soon they began to laugh at him, because he was not strong as well as kind.

After King Robert had reigned for two or three years, a great gloom slowly began to settle upon the country.

KING ROBERT AND THE POPE

Many people believed that a thousand years after the birth of Christ the world would come to an end. And now the time was drawing near.

The nobles were afraid, and wished to atone for all the wrong things they had done. They could think of no better way to do this than to give their lands, houses, slaves to the Church, and to go themselves on a pilgrimage to Palestine, where Jesus had lived and died.

The poorer folk left their fields untilled, unsown, for where was the need to plow and sow when before harvest time they might all have perished? Rich and poor alike crowded into the churches to confess their sins.

The dreaded year 1000 dawned at last, and, to the wonder of every one, the sun still rose day after day, and the world still went on its quiet way. Then, little by little, the people forgot their fears, and went back to their old selfish, thoughtless lives. But the Church had grown richer and more powerful during those last terrible months, and it had now a stronger hold than ever over the people.

King Robert was, as you know, devoted to the Church, yet he drew down her anger on himself and on his people. He had married a lady named Bertha, whom he dearly loved. Queen Bertha was a cousin of the king, and the Pope said that cousins were forbidden to marry one another. The king must therefore send his wife away, or incur the anger of the Church.

But King Robert loved Bertha too well to send her away, so the Pope excommunicated both the king and the queen. This was a terrible punishment, for to be excommunicated meant to be banished from the Church and all her sacraments, and to be shunned and forsaken by every good Catholic.

No sooner had the Pope pronounced his sentence of excommunication, than the king and queen were deserted by their court, and forced to live almost entirely alone. They found it difficult sometimes to get enough to eat, for all their servants had run away, save two poor slaves. Even they would not stay in the room with the king a moment longer than they could help, so great was the power of the Pope's curse.

But I have not yet told you the worst. As the king would not yield, the Pope next put the whole land under an Interdict or Ban.

An Interdict meant that all the churches were closed, that all the bells hung silent in the belfries, that the images of saints were taken down and laid upon beds of ashes and thorns, and that the pictures in the churches were covered up, although, as the churches were shut, there was no one to look at them.

As long as the Interdict lasted, no baptism service, no marriage service, could take place. The dead were buried as was needful, but no prayers were said over the grave.

Thus stricken and sad, the people suffered with their king.

King Robert, for all his gentle ways, defied the Pope for many weary weeks, but at length he could no longer bear to think of the sufferings of his people, and for their sake he sent Queen Bertha to a convent. And in the convent the poor queen often wept, for well she knew that never again would she see King Robert.

The Pope was triumphant. As for the king, he was at once taken back into the favor of the Church, and the Interdict was removed from the land. Then the doors of the churches were thrown wide open, and the bells rang joyful peals. The images, too, were put back in their niches, and the pictures were unveiled.

King Robert knew that he had made his people glad, but he never forgot Queen Bertha, not even when he married a beautiful lady called Constance, who unhappily was as cruel as she was beautiful.

Constance was the daughter of the Count of Toulouse,

KING ROBERT AND THE POPE

one of the greatest nobles of southern France. In her father's house she had ruled as a queen, and was both gay and haughty. She and her lords and ladies brought with them to Paris many new customs and new ways of dressing.

"Short hair, shaven chins, ridiculous boots turned up at the toes," such were some of the new fashions; while the strangers' "mode of living, their appearance, their armor, the harness of their horses, are," says an old writer, "all equally whimsical." It seemed too that these people "thought and spoke as strangely as they dressed."

As I told you, Queen Constance was a cruel woman. Through her influence the king too sometimes forgot his kindly ways.

Two priests, one of whom was the queen's own confessor, were charged with not believing all that the Pope said they ought to believe. This crime was called Heresy.

The king, urged by the queen, actually commanded that these two priests should be punished for their heresy by being burned alive.

As the two priests passed Constance on their way to the stake, the queen, it is said, thrust out one of her confessor's eyes with a small iron-tipped staff which she held in her hand.

This was the first time that Christians put other Christians to death for not believing all that the Pope said they ought to believe.

Constance had three sons. She taught these princes no reverence for their father the king, and when they grew up they rebelled, and at length even took up arms against him.

King Robert was strong enough to compel his sons to lay down their arms, but their conduct and his wife's cruelty broke his heart. He died in the year 1031. If his family were not grieved at his death, his subjects wept bitterly, because they had lost the king who had almost always been kind and gentle.

"Widows and orphans did beat their breasts and went to and from his tomb, crying, 'Whilst Robert was king and ordered all, we lived in peace, we had nought to fear. May his soul . . . mount up and and dwell for ever with Jesus Christ, the King of kings.'"

Thus, amid the tears and blessings of his people, Robert the Pious was laid to rest.

CHAPTER XIV

THE TRUCE OF GOD

QUEEN CONSTANCE's evil influence did not end when King Robert died.

Her youngest son Robert was her favorite, and she wished to see him on the throne of France. When therefore Henry, her eldest son, became king after his father's death, Constance was so angry that she did all she could to win the most powerful barons from their allegiance to Henry I. She succeeded so well that civil war broke out.

Henry I. determined to keep the crown that was his by right, and he begged the Duke of Normandy, a descendant of Rollo, to help him put down the rebellion which his mother had provoked.

Robert of Normandy at once came to the help of his king, and fought as his ancestors had fought of old, so valiantly, that ever after he was known as *Robert le Diable,* which means Robert the Devil.

Constance and her party were vanquished, and seeing that she had now nothing to gain by continuing to fight, the queen-mother made friends with her eldest son.

Henry I. showed that he could be generous, by forgiving his mother, and giving the title of Duke of Burgundy to his brother Robert, while the Duke of Normandy was rewarded for the help he had given to the king by the gift of large tracts of land which lay between the river Seine and the river Oise.

The war was over, but there was still great distress in the land. For three years the harvests had been growing poorer and poorer. Even the rich had little to eat, while the peasants were forced to satisfy their hunger with roots which they found in the forests. When these failed they devoured human flesh.

After famine came the plague, and so many hundreds of poor folk died, that before they could be buried wolves came out of the forests and feasted upon the bodies.

So great was the distress that the bishops and clergy of France met together to see if they could do anything to help the poor oppressed people. The barons were still grinding them down, and exacting more taxes than were their due from their hungry, plague-stricken vassals.

We do not hear that the bishops and priests were able to give food to those who were starving, but they did what they could when they said that the "Peace of God" was to be held sacred. The "Peace of God" forbade the nobles to take from the poor more taxes than were their due. It also forbade fighting and violence throughout the land.

But if at first the "Peace of God" made the nobles curb their angry passions, and behave less harshly toward the peasants, they soon forgot all about it, and slipped back to their usual fierce and cruel ways.

"The lords do us nought but ill," cried the peasants. "Every day is for us a day of suffering, toil and weariness; every day we have our cattle taken from us to work for our lords."

At length the peasants met together to find, if it were possible, a way out of their troubles.

"Why suffer all this evil to be done to us, and not get out of our plight?" they said to one another. "Are we not men even as our lords? Let us learn to resist the knight, and we shall be free to cut down trees, to hunt and fish after our fashion, aand we shall work our will in flood and field and wood."

Poor peasants! Their wants were so simple—just to be allowed to fish, to hunt, and to go into the woods to cut firewood.

THE TRUCE OF GOD 75

But when they ventured to send some of their number to the nobles to complain of their sufferings, and to tell their simple needs, listen to what was done.

The nobles were so angry that the peasants had dared to complain, that they cut off the hands and feet of their messengers. Then they sent them away, to go home as they could, and show to those who had sent them what they too might expect if they dared again to complain of the wrongs which they endured.

That such things could be done showed the bishops that the "Peace of God" had failed. They therefore now proclaimed the "Truce of God."

By the "Truce of God" they believed that at least certain days might be kept free from violence. It forbade any one to fight each week from Wednesday evening until Monday morning. Christmas Day, Easter, Lent, and indeed all the great saints' days were also set apart. And this proved of more use than the "Peace of God." The nobles, finding themselves forced to curb their angry passions on certain days, grew gradually less violent. Many of them laid aside their swords and brought their wealth to the altar, and then set out, either alone or in small companies, on a pilgrimage.

For already, in the year 1032, it had become a custom for those who were sorry for their sins to go to the Holy Land. If they might but touch the sepulcher in which the body of Jesus had lain, or spend a long night on the mount called Calvary, the pilgrims believed that all their sins would be forgiven.

Among the nobles who went to the Holy Land at this time was Robert, Duke of Normandy.

Before he set out the duke assembled the nobles of Normandy, and, lest he should not return, he appointed his little son William, who was then seven years old, to be their lord. This little boy became William the Great, Conqueror of England.

Duke Robert reached Jerusalem in safety, but on his way home he took ill and died.

At first the barons of Normandy refused to acknowledge William as their lord. Yet he was a manly lad, and had already begun to rule his compaions. At fifteen years of age he begged to be armed as a knight. When this was done, "it was a sight both pleasant and terrible to see him guiding his horse's career, flashing with his sword, gleaming with his shield, and threatening with his casque and javelin."

William could not subdue the rebellious barons alone, so he asked King Henry to come to his aid.

At first Henry helped the young duke, but afterwards, fearing lest William should grow too powerful, he went over to the side of the barons and fought against him.

But the young duke was brave and strong. His friends, too, were loyal and true. So when the armies of the king and of the duke met, Henry was utterly defeated, and never again ventured into William's lands with an army.

Two years after he had been defeated by William, Henry i. died, having done little for the good of his country.

CHAPTER XV

PETER THE HERMIT

IN this chapter I shall have more to tell you of a strange, ugly-looking little man called Peter the Hermit than of Henry's son, who now became Philip I.

Philip had been a lazy, selfish boy, and he grew up into a wicked, self-pleasing man. And so when the chance came to do a noble deed, an unselfish act, Philip thrust the opportunity from him, that he might live idly and undisturbed in his luxurious palaces.

When William of Normandy asked the king to join him in his great expedition to conquer England, Philip would have nothing to do with the plans of his ambitious vassal.

So William sailed for England with a great army, and, as you know from your English history, he fought and won the battle of Hastings, in 1066, against King Harold of England.

From that day the Norman duke became also the King of England.

Philip I. may now have been sorry that he had not joined William in his great enterprise. In any case he became jealous of his powerful vassal, and resolved when the opportunity arrived to injure him.

About nine years passed, and then the chance for which Philip was waiting came.

Robert, the son of William the Conqueror, was angry with his father because he had refused to make him governor of Normandy.

Philip I. was only too pleased to encourage Robert's anger, and to help him stir up rebellion in Normandy.

When William the Conqueror found out what Philip was doing he was very angry, and his anger was a thing to be feared. He at once went to war with his enemy, and had already taken one of Philip's towns and burned it to the ground, when, as he rode through the conquered city, his horse slipped on a burning cinder. King William was thrown forward on his horse, and was so badly hurt that six weeks later he died.

Philip I. was not sorry that the enemy he had provoked could trouble him no more. It was the easier for him to spend his time in pleasure and in idleness. And this he still did, while France, and indeed the whole of Europe, was being roused as by a trumpet call.

The Holy City, Jerusalem, had been for many years in the hands of the Turks. As you know, they were a fierce and cruel people, and imprisoned, tortured, and even killed, the pilgrims to Jerusalem.

At last Europe was roused to try to rescue the Holy City from the hands of these cruel people. The expeditions which set out from France, from England, from Germany, for this purpose, were called Crusades, and the people who took part in them the Crusaders. It is of the first crusade that I wish now to tell you. It was a strange little man who wandered through France, calling on the people to rouse themselves to set the Holy City free. Peter the Hermit, as he was called, was ugly and small, but the keen bright eyes that looked out of his thin pinched face seemed to see right into the hearts of those to whom he spoke. He was not old, this plain-looking little man, but he had suffered much, so that already his hair and beard were white.

The Hermit wore a woolen tunic, and over that a serge cloak, which reached to his feet. His arms and his feet

PETER THE HERMIT

were bare. Often he was to be seen riding on an ass, and holding in his hand a crucifix.

Peter had once journeyed to Jerusalem, and he had seen for himself how pilgrims were robbed by the Turks; how the places where Christ's blessed feet had trod were defiled by cruelty too great to be told.

So when Peter left Jerusalem he journeyed to Rome, his heart on fire with the evils he had seen and the wrongs he had borne in the Holy City. He was going to Rome to tell the Pope all that he had seen and suffered.

When the Pope, Urban II, had heard Peter's tale, he blessed him, bidding him go from town to town, from land to land, to tell all who would hear of the things he had seen in Jerusalem.

Thus it was that in 1094 the First Crusade began to be preached.

At first but a few came to hear Peter speak. There was nothing about the plain-looking little man to make them come. But the few who listened to his words soon brought others to hear, and gradually crowds gathered wherever Peter went. For this man, so small, so plain, had a great gift from God, the gift of speech.

When Peter spoke, his words fell as fire upon the hearts of those who pressed around him. As he told of all that he had seen in Jerusalem, the people almost believed that they were in Jerusalem, seeing the very sights Peter had seen. His words were indeed as a fire, and kindled in the hearts of the people a flame that did not die even when in very truth they stood at the gates of the Holy City.

For a year Peter went through France rousing the people. Then in 1095 many of those who had listened to him journeyed to a town called Clermont, where the Pope, Urban II, was now going to hold a great Council.

The days were already cold and wintry, for it was November when the people crowded into Clermont. Soon all the houses in the town were full, as well as those in the villages round about. And still the people came in great numbers. Many of them were forced to put up tents in the meadows, where they would have been cold indeed, save for the fire which Peter had kindled in their hearts.

In an open space in the center of the town a platform was erected. Here, on a certain day, in the midst of a great throng of people, stood the Pope, with Peter the Hermit by his side.

"Men of France," cried Urban ii, "right valiant knights . . . it is from you above all that Jerusalem hopes for help. Take part in this Holy War, I beseech you, and all your sins will be forgiven." Peter also talked to the people, telling them yet again of all the misery that Christians in Jerusalem suffered, until at length a great shout went up from the hearts of the people. "God willeth it! God willeth it!" they cried, and these words became the battle-cry of the crusaders.

Then from the Pope's own hands the people received the sign or badge of their great undertaking. There was but one sign fitting for such a warfare, the sign of the Cross. This was made of red silk or cloth, and was fastened on the crusader's cloak, or on the front of his helmet.

The Pope was a wise man, and he knew that it would take many months for a great army to get ready to march to Jerusalem, so he said that the first crusade should not start until about nine months later, in August, 1096.

But although the knights were ready to wait until they had made preparations for their long and difficult journey, the mob clamored to be led to the Holy City by Peter without further delay. And Peter and one poor knight, called Walter the Penniless, yielded to these foolish people. These crusaders, however, were not an army, but only a vast rabble of men, women and children, who were all unprepared for the long and difficult journey to Palestine.

Peter the Hermit, it is true, knew the way to the Holy Land, but he forgot how difficult it would be to feed so great a multitude, and how impossible it would be for these poor folks to wrest the Holy Sepulcher from the Turks, if they ever reached Jerusalem.

The mob set out in great joy, but it was not long before the hardships of the journey began to make them grumble. They grew hungry, for Peter had not stayed to take provisions for so great a company. In their hunger they grew desperate, and when they reached a town they would plunder it, as though they were a band of robbers rather than pilgrims of the Holy Cross.

Thousands who set out died upon the way, of hunger or disease, while many more who reached Hungary were slain by the wild tribes who dwelt in that land.

At length Peter, with those of his company who were left, reached Constantinople. Here they took ship and crossed the Bosphorus into Asia Minor, only to be met by the Turks, who attacked them so fiercely that Peter was left with scarcely three thousand followers.

We hear no more of these poor people until Peter, and those who had not died from hunger or sickness, joined the real crusading army when at length it entered Asia Minor.

Meanwhile, the knights of France had assembled two great armies to fight in the Holy War. The nobles themselves sold their houses, their lands, their treasures, that they might have money to equip and feed their army.

Philip I. knew what his nobles were doing, but he neither helped nor hindered them. His own pleasures were engrossing all his time and thought.

The two French armies were joined by a third formed of Norman knights who had settled in Italy. The three armies were led by nobles who had already won renown on the field of battle.

Godfrey de Bouillon was one of these leaders. His father had been a warrior, his mother a saint, and those who watched Godfrey would say of him, "For zeal in war behold his father, for serving God behold his mother." And they said this because they believed that this knight was warrior and saint in one.

Tancred, "a very gentle perfect knight," was another of the leaders of the first crusade.

The third and oldest of these great leaders was Raymond, Count of Toulouse. He had vowed that he would never return to France, but would stay in the east fighting the Turks as long as he lived in order to atone for his many sins.

It was a great host that at last, in August, 1096, set out for the Holy Land. It had many hardships to suffer from famine and disease before it reached Asia Minor.

As soon as they landed, however, the crusaders determined to attack Nicæa without delay. Nicæa was an important town belonging to the Turks.

As they marched toward this town, they met Peter the Hermit, followed by a small band of pilgrims. This band was all that was left of the vast rabble that had set out from France in 1096.

Peter told the leaders of the real crusade all that had befallen him and his followers, and then gladly joined the army for which he had been looking and longing for many weary months.

Nicæa was reached and at once besieged. The town was in the hands of a Turkish sultan called Kilidj Arslan.

When the sultan had heard that the crusaders were drawing near, he had gone to assemble all his forces. His wife, his children, and his treasures he had left in the town. He had also sent a message to the people, bidding them "be of good courage, and fear not the barbarous people who make show of besieging our city. To-morrow, before the seventh hour of the day, ye shall be delivered from your enemies."

The sultan did all he could to make his words come true. On the following day he arrived before the walls of his city with a large force, and fell upon the besieging army. The crusaders fought bravely, Godfrey de Bouillon leading them on with the courage for which he was renowned. He himself killed a Turk, "remarkable amongst all for his size and strength," and whose arrows had been causing great havoc in the ranks of the crusading armies. Kilidj Arslan was defeated, and withdrew from Nicæa to find a fresh army.

For six weeks the crusaders besieged the sultan's town; and then, just when they believed it was ready to surrender to them, they saw waving from its towers the flag of the Greek emperor.

Now the Emperor Alexis had seemed to befriend the crusaders, but during the siege he had sent secret messages to the inhabitants of Nicæa, persuading them to yield to him. And this the people of Nicæa had done the more willingly because they had once belonged to the Greek empire, and Alexis had promised not to treat them as a conquered people, but as those who had returned to their former masters.

The crusaders were sorely disappointed, for they had hoped to plunder the town, while their leaders were wroth because the Emperor Alexis would allow not more than ten of their number to enter Nicæa at the same time. But it was useless to show the Greek emperor that he had angered them, so the knights determined to march on towards the south-east of Asia Minor, and thus to reach Syria.

In order to get provisions the more easily the vast army of the crusaders now divided into two.

One morning as Tancred led his host forward, it was suddenly attacked by a great number of Turks, who poured down upon it from the neighboring hills. These Turkish hordes were led by Kilidj Arslan, who had followed the crusaders after the fall of Nicæa, and had now taken them by surprise.

The Duke of Normandy, who was with Tancred, rushed

into the fray, waving his gold and white banner, and shouting, "God willeth it! God willeth it!" Another knight hastily sent a message to Godfrey de Bouillon, who was not yet far away, to come to their aid. Godfrey, with about fifty knights, galloped on before the main body of his army, and, joining Tancred, flung himself upon the enemy.

By noon Godfrey's whole army arrived, with trumpets blowing and flags waving. Kilidj Arslan began to think he would retreat, but his retreat was speedily turned to flight. For the crusaders pursued the Turks so fiercely that they fled in terror, and "two days afterwards they were still flying though none pursued them, unless it were God Himself."

After this victory the crusaders marched on toward Syria, but for the future they determined to keep together.

The armies had now to cross great tracts of deserted country, where neither food nor water was to be found, where there was no shelter from the burning sun.

Not only the soldiers but the horses suffered terribly and died in hundreds, and many of the knights were forced to ride on asses or oxen. These animals were hardier, and better able to stand the heat than the horses. And the heat was terrible, and made the whole army suffer more than even from lack of water.

One day the dogs that usually followed the army disappeared for some hours. When they came back their paws were wet.

The soldiers noticed the wet paws with joy, for they knew that the dogs must have found water, and without delay they set out to look for it. You can imagine with what delight the poor thirsty men at last discovered a small river, how eagerly they drank, and how they ran to tell their comrades the good news.

I may not stop to tell you of all the towns the crusaders besieged on their way to Jerusalem, nor of all that they suffered, but in the spring of 1099 the great army really entered Palestine, and, in June of the same year, it at length caught sight of the Holy City.

"Lo! Jerusalem appears in sight. Lo! every hand points out Jerusalem. Lo! a thousand voices are heard as one in salutation of Jerusalem."

Thus, says the Italian poet Tasso, was the army moved at the sight of the Holy City.

After this first glimpse of the city neither the knights nor the rough soldiers dared to raise their eyes to look upon her, so great was their awe.

"In accents of humility, with words low-spoken, with stifled sobs, with sighs and tears, the pent-up yearnings of a people in joy and at the same time in sorrow, sent shivering through the air a murmur like that which is heard in leafy forests what time the wind blows through the leaves, or like the dull sound made by the sea which breaks upon the rocks, or hisses as it foams over the beach."

Jerusalem was in the hands of a large Turkish army, and the crusaders at once besieged the city.

Five weeks later she was theirs. Then alas! mad with triumph, the crusaders forgot that they were soldiers of the Cross. They slew the helpless inhabitants of the city; they plundered the houses and churches.

But soon they grew ashamed of their cruel deeds, and flinging aside their armor they clothed themselves in white robes. Then in shame and sorrow the crusaders climbed the hill of Calvary.

Jerusalem was taken on July 15, 1099, and about a week later the leaders of the crusade met together to choose a king to rule over the Holy City.

Robert, Duke of Normandy, was the first to be proposed.

"But he refused, liking better to give himself up to repose and indolence in Normandy, than to serve as a soldier the King of kings; for which God never forgave him."

Tancred was then asked to accept the great charge. But he wished for no higher rank than was already his.

Raymond, Count of Toulouse, was too old, and said that he "would have a horror of bearing the name of king in Jerusalem."

Godfrey de Bouillon did not wish to be king, yet being chosen not only by Tancred and the Count of Toulouse, but by all the other knights of the crusading army, he accepted the trust, although he refused to take the title of King. He would be called only "Defender and Baron of the Holy Sepulcher." Nor would he wear a crown. "I will never wear a crown of gold in the place where the Savior of the world was crowned with thorns," said the great knight, as simply as a child.

Thus, with the taking of Jerusalem, ended the first crusade.

Meanwhile, Philip I. was growing, as slothful people will ever do, more slothful.

His son Louis was now twenty-two years of age, and Philip thought it would be pleasant to lay the burden of kingship upon the shoulders of his son, and perhaps it was the wisest thing he could have done.

So Louis was crowned king, and Philip was free to live his own indolent life to the end.

But before he died Philip grew sorry for all the wrong he had done, and for all the good he had left undone. And to show that he was really sorry he did public penance as the priests decreed. He also began to give alms to the poor. In 1108 Philip I. died, and by his own wish he was buried in a quiet little church on the river Loire, rather than in the abbey of St. Denis, where the kings of France were laid to rest. For at the end of his life Philip I. knew himself to have been unworthy of the name of king, and even in death he wished to humble himself in the eyes of his people.

CHAPTER XVI

THE ORIFLAMME

The time of which I have been telling you, from the death of Charlemange to the beginning of the reign of Louis the Fat, is known as the Dark Ages. And you will scarcely be surprised that these centuries should have so gloomy a name. For you have read of the wars of the kings, the rebellions of the nobles. You have heard how the lords ground down their vassals and trampled on their slaves, who were sold with the land as carelessly as a plow or a spade might be sold. You have seen, too, how the peasants, daring to tell the nobles of their misery, were punished by having their hands and feet cut off. It is well that the times when such things took place should be known as the Dark Ages.

But from the time of Louis the Fat the darkness began, little by little, to grow less dense. Louis himself began to lighten the darkness.

In spite of his great size, which made his people call him "the Fat," Louis vi. was no sluggard. He was indeed also called "the Fighter," because his body was so active; "the Wideawake," because his mind was so quick.

In Philip's listless hands the king's power had grown less, his dominions fewer. So now, though Louis was called King of France, he owned only five cities and the lands belonging to them. His power, too, scarcely reached beyond these five cities.

From Paris to St. Denis the road was safe, but farther

even the king could not travel without a strong bodyguard to protect him.

The barons had built great towers with gloomy dungeons along the highways, and as travelers passed they with their men-at-arms would sally forth, and take prisoners all whom they could. After robbing their captives the barons threw them into dungeons. Here they were often tortured until, in order to be set free, they promised to pay enormous sums of money.

Louis made up his mind that the barons should be punished, and more than that, that their power should be taken away.

To help him in this great work he had a friend who was also his prime minister. This was Suger, Abbot of St. Denis, with whom Louis had been educated.

The king himself had not many troops for his great undertaking. There were only his vassals and three hundred brave youths who had come to Paris, hoping to win their spurs in the service of their king.

But Suger and many other abbots and priests roused the peasants and townsfolk, and themselves led these rough troops to Louis's aid. The clergy were only too glad to fight against the barons, who had treated them with but scant courtesy, and had often robbed their monasteries and churches.

Thus, aided by the priests, Louis gradually cleared the highways of the robber bands, and forced the barons to live quietly in their castles. If they dared to disobey him he attacked their strongholds.

One of the most powerful of the barons was Hugh the Fair. He had trampled on the peasants and treated them worse than his dogs, until they hated him with all the strength they had.

When at length a priest led a band of these peasants against Hugh's castle, their anger against the noble was so terrible that Hugh might well wish himself far away.

THE ORIFLAMME

Strong walls, iron gates, nothing would have kept the peasants out. But the priest who led them found a weak spot in the fortress, and through this the peasants crept within the walls, and Hugh and his followers were at the mercy of the mob.

King Louis meanwhile was attacking the castle at another point; and Hugh, fighting desperately, escaped from the mob, and surrendered himself to the king. Hugh's castle was plundered and then pulled to pieces, and he himself rendered harmless. And what befell Hugh the Fair befell many other barons throughout France.

The people, finding themselves freed from the worst oppressions of the nobles, were grateful to the king, and learned to love him well. As for the townsfolk, many of them were rewarded for their share in the struggle by being allowed to choose their own magistrates, to make their own laws, and to carry a standard or banner of their own choosing before them into battle. The towns to which Louis granted these liberties were called Communes.

In 1124, while he was still working for the good of his kingdom, Louis was threatened with war. Henry I. of England had made an alliance against France with his son-in-law the Emperor of Germany. The emperor had set out meaning to invade the east of France and to attack Rheims, the city in which the French kings were crowned.

Louis, nothing daunted, called together his vassals and commanded the barons to come with their troops to his aid. Many of the barons, having had proof of Louis's power to compel obedience, obeyed his summons. Others, who did not dare to refuse, took care to come too late to be of any use had a battle been fought.

When the soldiers had assembled, Louis went to the abbey of St. Denis for the Oriflamme, which was the national banner of France, and carried it to the head of his army. There it waved, a banner of flame-red silk, edged with green, fastened to a rod of gold.

As the French word for gold is *or,* you will now understand the first part of the big name by which the banner was called. The other part *flamme* is our word flame.

But after all these preparations no battle was fought. For the German emperor, hearing of the great army which Louis the Fighter had assembled, and disturbed also by rumors of rebellion in one of his own German towns, first ordered his army to halt, and then ordered it to march back to Germany.

Soon after this the German emperor died, and peace was made with Henry I, King of England. The Oriflamme, brought with so much solemnity from St. Denis, was then taken back and laid once more on the altar of the abbey.

In 1129 Louis's eldest son, Philip, was crowned king. Louis hoped that Philip would soon be able to help him to govern the kingdom. But two years later an accident shattered his hopes. For Philip, who was now sixteen years old, was riding in the streets of Paris, which at that time were both narrow and dirty, when a pig, "a diabolical pig" Suger calls it, got between the legs of his horse, and both the prince and the animal fell to the ground.

Philip was so badly hurt that he died the same night.

When the king knew that his son was dead his grief was terrible. He shut himself up alone, and for days refused to take any interest in his people.

About a fortnight after his brother's death King Louis's second boy was crowned king. Six years later, in 1137, Louis died, and his young son came to the throne.

Suger, the Abbot of St. Denis, tells us that when Louis VI. was ill he was carried on a litter to St. Denis, where he had hoped to die. "As he went," says the abbot, "all men ran together from castle and town, or from the plow-tail in the field, to meet him and show their devotion to the king who had protected them and given them peace."

In the reign of Louis VI. the schools of Paris grew famous. One of the greatest teachers in these schools was Abelard, a man of great eloquence and a famous scholar. Many people journeyed from distant lands to Paris for the sake of listening to this wonderful teacher.

With the name of Abelard is joined the name of Héloïse, one of his pupils, whom he dearly loved.

Héloïse, although she loved Abelard, became a nun at his bidding, but when she died she was laid in the tomb where her master had been buried. The letters which they wrote to one another in Latin are so beautiful that they are still read with delight.

CHAPTER XVII

THE SECOND CRUSADE

Louis VII. was called "the Young," because he was only eighteen when he began to reign, but the name clung to him until he died at the age of sixty.

Suger, the Abbot of St. Denis, who had been the friend and minister of Louis VI., had also been the tutor of the young king.

When Louis the Young was grown to be a man, Suger still had great influence over him, and it was really the abbot who ruled the kingdom.

But though Suger had great power, he lived quite quietly and simply in a tiny cell in the abbey of St. Denis. His bed was of straw, his bedclothes only a rough woolen counterpane. If any one visited the abbot in his cell, he would not have seen the rough couch upon which Suger slept, for through the day it was carefully covered with a carpet.

By his father's wish Louis the Young had married Eleanor, a rich princess whose father ruled Aquitaine in the south of France, as well as many other wealthy provinces. As her dowry she brought both her lands and wealth to the young king.

But though the princess was rich, she was so different in character from Louis, that it was not easy for either of them to live happily together.

Queen Eleanor was gay, ambitious, selfish; while Louis, trained by the devout Abbot of St. Denis, was grave, humble, and unselfish.

THE SECOND CRUSADE

About five years after he began to reign, Louis the Young went to war with one of his barons. The king's soldiers set fire to Vitry, the town which they were besieging. As it was built of wood the flames spread to the church, in which the inhabitants of the town had taken refuge. When the poor people saw that they would be burned to death, they uttered piercing cries, and these cries reached the ear of the king.

Had it been possible Louis would even then have saved the people, but the flames had spread so quickly that it was too late to do anything, and they all perished.

The king could never forget the cries he had heard, and blamed himself for what had happened. He determined to do penance for this and all his other sins by going on a pilgrimage.

At this very time St. Bernard, the great and holy Abbot of Clairvaux, was going from city to city throughout France rousing the people, even as Peter the Hermit had done, to go on a crusade against the Turks.

Edessa, one of the great strongholds of the Christians in the east, had been captured by the Turks, who had then cruelly massacred the inhabitants. These tidings reached France while St. Bernard was preaching the Second Crusade. It added to the power of his words as he cried, "Christian warriors, He who gave His life for you to-day demandeth yours."

King Louis heard, and believed that this was the penance for which he had been seeking. The multitude, too, who listened shouted the old battle-cry of the crusaders, "God willeth it! God willeth it!"

Then Louis, kneeling at the feet of St. Bernard, took from his hand the Cross, the badge of the Holy War. Knight after knight followed the king's example. The people also clamored for "Crosses, Crosses," until St. Bernard tore up his garments that the pieces might be made into badges for the eager multitude.

From France the abbot, still preaching the crusade, journeyed into Germany.

The Emperor, Conrad III., was not as easily persuaded to join the movement as St. Bernard wished. Conrad believed, and perhaps truly, that his own kingdom needed his presence.

Then one day, when the emperor was present in church, St. Bernard drew a picture of Jesus bearing His cross and reproaching Conrad because he had not helped Him to carry it.

The emperor, as he listened, was strangely moved. He interrupted the preacher, crying, "I know what I owe to Jesus Christ, and I swear to go whither it pleaseth Him to call me."

And so in 1147, when the second crusade set out for Palestine, Louis VII. and Conrad III. were each at the head of a large army.

Conrad reached Asia Minor first. Before Louis could join him the Turks had fallen upon the German army and utterly defeated it. Those who escaped joined the French army, and together they began to march across Asia Minor. But Conrad went back to Constantinople.

King Louis gained a great victory over the Turks close to the river Meander, but soon after his army got scattered and lost among the narrow passes of the mountains in Pisidia.

The Turks had foreseen that this would happen, and were awaiting the scattered army as it struggled in small companies out of the narrow mountain passes.

Louis's bodyguard was slain before his eyes. The king, left alone, placed himself against a rock, and fought with his sword so desperately, that at length the Turks who had attacked him turned and fled. Had they known it was the king, they might have been less ready to leave their prize.

When the Turks had fled, Louis, glancing round, saw close at hand a riderless horse. He lost not a moment in

THE SECOND CRUSADE

mounting it, and galloping off he soon rejoined his advanced guard, who had feared that their king was slain.

The army now continued its march until it arrived at a small seaport on the Mediterranean. King Louis had hoped to reach Antioch by land. But to march there would still take forty days, and food was scarce, while to go by sea would take only three days.

Unfortunately it was impossible to provide ships for the whole army. At first King Louis refused to desert those who had followed him so far, but before long he was persuaded to embark with as many knights as the ships would hold, and the army was left to its fate.

Before he sailed the king gave all the money and provisions he had to the soldiers to help them on their long and dangerous march to Antioch. But only a remnant of the army ever set out on that march. For no sooner had the king and his nobles sailed than the Turks fell upon the forsaken soldiers, and many of them were slain or taken prisoners.

When Louis reached Antioch in March 1148, he heard of the terrible fate that had overtaken his army; and again, as when the people of Vitry were burned, he felt that he was responsible for the terrible disaster.

In April King Louis reached Jerusalem, where the Emperor Conrad, disguised as a pilgrim, also arrived accompanied by only a few knights. Soon afterward the remnant of the French and German armies joined their kings, who at once determined to lay siege to Damascus.

But the town was too strong to be taken by the feeble force which was now all that was left of the united armies. The siege was raised, and the king and the emperor went back to Jerusalem. Conrad, discouraged and disappointed, returned to Germany soon after the siege of Damascus had been raised.

Louis could not make up his mind to go home. He had done so little, and lost so large a part of his army, that he was ashamed to face his faithful minister Suger. Gradually many of the knights went back to France, but Louis lingered in Jerusalem.

At length the entreaties of Suger, who had sent messengers to beg the king to come home, were successful, and in the autumn of 1149 Louis was once more in France. Of the great army with which he had set out for Palestine, only two or three hundred knights were left to journey home with the king.

Suger, who had been regent during the king's absence, welcomed him with joy, and, having given Louis an account of his work, retired to St. Denis. Here he spent the rest of his life, ruling his abbey as wisely as he had ruled the kingdom of France.

Three years after Louis's return from the crusade Suger died. The king missed his minister sorely, but perhaps the kingdom missed his strong hand even more. Louis had called Suger the Father of the Country, and in the years to come it was by this name that he was long remembered.

A few months after Suger's death Queen Eleanor left Louis to marry Henry Plantagenet, Count of Anjou. She brought to her new husband the rich provinces of Aquitaine and Poitou.

A chronicler who lived in Anjou at this time, and ought to have known the count, tells us that he was "vigorous in war, marvelous in prudence of reply, frugal in habits, munificent to others, sober, kindly, peaceable. He bore himself so wisely, defended himself so manfully, that all men, even his foes, praised him."

It was this worthy count who became Henry II, King of England. And you can easily understand that Louis was not at all pleased that so powerful a ruler as the King of England should also possess so many rich provinces in France.

From 1154, when Henry Plantagenet became King of England, the struggle between him and Louis never ended.

THE SECOND CRUSADE

And long after Henry II. and Louis VII. had ceased to reign, the struggle between the two countries was continued, until at length an English king laid claim to the throne of France.

Meanwhile Louis, forsaken by Eleanor, married again. His second wife, however, died in 1160. Then Louis married a third time, and in 1165 a son was born, heir to the throne of France.

The little prince was named Philip, but the people in their gladness called him *Dieu donné,* the Gift of God.

When Philip was fifteen years old the king wished his son to be crowned. The day before the coronation, however, Philip went out to hunt and lost himself in a forest. Cold and bewildered, he wandered about all night, and only in the morning did he find his way back to the palace.

Unfortunately the prince had caught cold during the night in the forest, and soon he grew so ill, Louis feared that his son would die.

Then the king did a strange thing. He left the prince lying ill in bed, and went to England on a pilgrimage to the tomb of Thomas à Becket.

When Thomas à Becket had been archbishop, King Louis had befriended him. Perhaps he hoped that now the archbishop had become a saint he would plead with God that the little sick Prince of France might get well.

At the end of five days, so quickly had Louis journeyed, he was back at the bedside of his son, who was already much better.

But the king himself, worn out with anxiety and the haste of the journey, took ill, and was unable to be present at the coronation of the prince.

During his illness he begged that all his money and his garments might be brought to him. Then with his own royal hands he divided both money and clothes among the poor, who by his request had been brought into the room where he lay.

In September 1180, a few months after the coronation of his son, Louis VII. died.

CHAPTER XVIII

ARTHUR, PRINCE OF NORMANDY, DISAPPEARS

PHILIP II. was only fifteen years old when he began to reign. He was a proud, ambitious boy, and eager to use his kingly power. He had often dreamed that he would make France as great as it had been in the time of Charlemange. His courtiers, and those of his people who knew his ambition, called him Philip Augustus, which meant Philip the Great, or the Imperial. Others named him Augustus for no other reason than that he was born in the month of August.

Like his grandfather, Louis the Fat, Philip wished to make the nobles less powerful, although indeed they had now fewer privileges than when Louis came to the throne.

The Duke of Burgundy had, however, provoked the young king. Philip therefore attacked one of his castles, and took his eldest son prisoner.

When the duke was at length compelled to ask for peace, Philip would grant it only on certain harsh conditions. The duke, not being powerful enough to fight against his sovereign, was forced to agree to whatever terms the king chose to impose. Whereupon Philip, who after all was but a boy, was so pleased to get his own way that he said, "The duke shall be my friend without any conditions," and he then at once repealed the harsh terms he had made shortly before.

Philip's chief friend was Richard, the son of Henry II, King of England.

Now Richard might be a good friend, but he was a bad

son. He took up arms against his father, and the French king encouraged him to rebel.

Philip himself attacked Aquitaine, which Henry II. had entrusted to Richard's care. Richard proved faithless to his trust, doing little to defend his father's province. It even seemed that he was going to hand it over to Philip. But before this had happened Henry made peace with the French king, and the English prince was saved from a treacherous deed.

After peace had been made between the two kings, Richard hastened to Philip's camp, lived in the same tent as the king, sat at his table, and even, it is said, slept in the same bed.

Again and again Henry and Philip were on the point of war, but again and again war was put off, while the kings met to settle their disputes under an ancient elm tree which stood on the boundary between France and Normandy.

At one of these meetings Philip and Henry forgot, for a time, their own quarrels. For terrible tidings had come from the east.

Since Godfrey de Bouillon had been elected King of Jerusalem after the first crusade, eight kings had reigned. These eight kings were each French, and the last one had now in 1187 been taken prisoner by the dreaded Saladin, and Jerusalem was once again in the hands of the Turks.

It was early in January 1188 that Philip and Henry, meeting under the elm tree, forgot their own quarrels, and spoke only of the need of a new crusade to deliver the Holy City from the hands of the Infidels. Before they separated the kings had agreed to make preparations to set out on the third crusade.

Unfortunately Philip and Henry soon began to think of their own disputes. The French king indeed grew so impatient, that in a fit of passion he cut down the ancient elm tree, saying he would hold no more meetings for

PRINCE OF NORMANDY DISAPPEARS

peace beneath its branches. Before the year 1188 ended, war broke out between the two kings.

But Henry II, deserted by his nobles and betrayed by his sons, was soon forced to ask for peace. Philip's terms were hard, for Henry II. was forced to own himself the French king's vassal, to yield to him the duchy of Berri, which lay south of the river Loire, and to promise to pardon all those who had betrayed him.

When the list of traitors was handed to the king, the first name was that of his own son John. Henry had loved John and forgiven him much, but this new treachery broke his heart, and he fell ill and died.

Richard now became King of England, and before long Philip and he had ceased to be friends. For in the third crusade, which set out in 1189, led by Philip Augustus and Richard, the English king was so brave that he became the hero of the armies, and won his well-known name of Cœur de Lion, the Lion-hearted. Then Philip grew jealous of Richard and returned to France, leaving part of his army to help his rival to carry on the war in the east.

Before he left Philip solemnly promised that, during Richard's absence, he would not attack his kingdom or harm him in any way. As he journeyed home, however, he asked the Pope to release him from his promise. The Pope refused, but Philip was no sooner back in France than he hastened to make friends with Prince John, who in his brother's absence was treacherously doing all he could to win the crown for himself.

Richard meanwhile had reached Palestine, and was within sight of Jerusalem. But knowing he had not an army strong enough to take the city, he covered his face with his cloak, refusing to look upon her, since he was unable to deliver her from her foes.

Soon afterwards he fell sick, and so making a treaty with the sultan, which secured the safety of pilgrims traveling to Jerusalem, he set out, by sea, for England.

Being shipwrecked he tried to cross Austria in disguise, for the Archduke of Austria was his enemy. He was, however, discovered and taken prisoner. The duke sold his royal captive to the Emperor of Germany for a large sum of money, and by the emperor Richard was thrown into prison.

When Philip knew that Richard was a prisoner he at once, in spite of his promise, attacked Normandy, of which province Richard was duke. It was bad enough that Philip should do this; it was surely even worse that Prince John, Richard's own brother, should help him. Together, too, they offered the German emperor large sums of money if he would but keep his royal captive safe.

But you have read the story of how a minstrel, called Blondel, who loved Richard, went in search of his king, and at last found out his prison. And you remember how he came back and told the English, who at once paid a heavy ransom that Richard might be set free.

Then indeed Philip and Prince John had cause to fear. Even the German emperor took the trouble to tell them to beware, for, said he, "the Devil is unchained," and by the Devil he meant no other than Richard the Lion-hearted.

Prince John was a coward as well as a traitor, and he hastened to make peace with his brother.

Richard had still, however, to deal with Philip.

He had reached England in 1194, and soon after his return he set out for Normandy with a large army.

The war with Philip lasted several years. Richard besieged a few towns, and fought a few unimportant battles. Then one day, in the year 1199, as he was besieging a castle, a soldier shot an arrow at random from the castle wall. The arrow wounded Richard, and ten days later he died. Philip had no longer anything to fear from his powerful rival.

Prince John at once caused himself to be proclaimed King of England and Duke of Normandy.

PRINCE OF NORMANDY DISAPPEARS

But he was not able to take possession of Normandy peaceably, for Arthur, a nephew of his own, claimed the province, and Philip, fearing lest the King of England should grow too powerful, gladly supported Prince Arthur's claim.

The people of Normandy had no love for John, so they sided with his nephew the prince, and Philip was thus easily able to proclaim Arthur, Duke of Normandy.

Soon after this King John succeeded in taking his nephew prisoner. For a short time Prince Arthur lay in a dungeon, wondering how he could escape from his cruel uncle.

Then one day, so it is said, King John came to take the prince out in a boat on the river Seine. The young lad was glad to leave his dungeon and live in the sunlight once again. He was pleased, too, that his uncle was kind. But before they had rowed far, King John suddenly drew his sword and stabbed his nephew, throwing the body into the river.

It may be that King John did not do this cruel deed, but the young prince was never seen again. Philip believed John was guilty, and summoned him, as Duke of Normandy and therefore his vassal, to appear before him. But King John paid no heed to the French king's summons. He was therefore tried, even though he was not present in the court, and found guilty of murder, and Normandy was declared to be his no longer.

King Philip then once more invaded Normandy; but John, though he was in the town of Rouen, took no notice of Philip's movements. He was lazy, and his courtiers were gay, so they idled their time until Philip's army actually reached the gates of Rouen.

Then indeed King John bestirred himself, not to fight but to flee, as quickly as might be, to England.

Thus the French king was left to take possession of Normandy, which therefore in 1204 became a part of the kingdom of France. And so wisely did Philip treat the Normans that they were content to own him as their king.

CHAPTER XIX

THE BATTLE OF BOUVINES

About four years after Normandy had become part of France, a great crusade was undertaken by the French. This crusade was not, as you would expect, to go to the east, or to fight against Saracens. It was to go to the beautiful provinces in the south of France; it was to war against French people. For in the fair provinces of Languedoe, Provence, Aquitaine, the people were, so the Pope declared, heretics; that is, they were enemies of the Pope, and worshiped God in other ways than did those who belonged to the Church of Rome. These heretics were called Albigensians. They lived careless, happy lives in the sunny south of France. But in 1208 they were roughly roused from their happiness.

The Pope, Innocent III., had ordered the nobles of France to put on the Cross, collect an army, and go slay the Albigensians, as though they were Turks nad Infidels.

So great was the army which assembled for this cruel crusade, that an old chronicler tells us, "From near and far they come; there be men from . . . Burgundy, France and Limousin; there be men from all the world. Never did God make scribe who, whatsoever his pains, could set them all down in writing, in two months or in three."

Into the south this countless army poured, led by Simon de Montfort, the father of the Simon de Montfort of whom you have read in your English history in the time of Henry III.

This Simon de Montfort was a fierce and cruel soldier, and the men under his control were allowed to do wicked

THE BATTLE OF BOUVINES

and cruel deeds. They had no care for women or little children, but killed them as readily as they killed strong men. They laid waste the beautiful province of Languedoc, and burnt all her villages.

Raymond, Count of Toulouse, one of the nobles of the south, did all he could to help the Albigensians. But his army was small compared with that of the crusaders; moreover, the Pope showed his displeasure by excommunicating the Count. Raymond then submitted to Innocent III., and before the war was over he was forced to join the crusaders, and even to lead them against his own people.

The town of Beziers was one of the strongholds of the heretics. It was attacked by Simon de Montfort and taken. Then the city was burnt, and every person in it was slain. Yet the inhabitants were not all heretics. There were many whom the Pope would have called true believers. One of the knights of the crusading army, anxious to spare whom he could, asked an abbot how he might know the true believers from the heretics. "Kill them all," was the brutal answer; "God will know His own."

This Albigensian crusade, begun, as I told you, in 1208, lasted for nearly twenty years. In 1218, however, as Simon de Montfort was besieging the town of Toulouse, a large stone, shot from the walls, hit the cruel captain and crushed him to death. When the Albigensians knew that their great enemy was dead, they roused themselves to a tremendous effort, and drove the crusaders out of their provinces. Thus for a time the war was at an end.

King Philip had not joined in the war against the Albigensians, but he had looked on, well pleased to see that the power of the nobles in the south was being weakened.

As a boy, you remember, Philip had dreamed that he would make France great, as it had been in the days of Charlemagne, and that he would spoil the insolence and power of the nobles. He had now added Normandy to the French crown, and been welcomed by the barons as her king. He had also seen the powerful nobles in the south of France beaten and stripped of their possessions by the crusading army. But Philip was not yet content. Why should he not conquer England, where King John was hated by his subjects? So he assembled a large army, and was ready to sail when the Pope interfered. For King John had begged for the Pope's protection, and had promised to pay a yearly tribute to Rome if he would save the country from the French.

As John had promised to pay tribute, the Pope looked on him as his vassal, and on England as his own. Philip was forbidden to invade the land. The French king was indignant that his plans should be disturbed, but he had no wish to incur the Pope's anger. Instead of sailing to England, Philip therefore led his army into Flanders in order to punish Ferrand, the count of that province. For when Philip had summoned the count, as his vassal, to help him invade England, Ferrand had refused to have anything to do with the war.

On the approach of Philip, the German emperor, Otho IV., a nephew of King John, and also a large number of English knights and archers, joined the Flemish.

Before the battle Otho assembled his men and said, "It is against Philip himself, and him alone, that we must direct all our efforts; it is he who must be slain first of all, for it is he alone who opposes us and makes himself our foe in everything. When he is dead, you will be able to divide the kingdom according to our pleasure." And then the emperor promised the Count of Flanders that when they had won the day he should have Paris for his prize.

Philip on his side was supported by many brave men. William des Barras, most famous of all brave knights, was there; while bishops used to handle the sword were on the battlefield among his followers. Many Commune towns also sent their trained bands of citizen soldiers to help

THE BATTLE OF BOUVINES

their king in his struggle against Germany, Flanders, and England.

The two armies marched through Flanders, and on Sunday, August 27, 1214, Philip reached Bouvines, not far from Tournay.

At Bouvines there was a bridge across the river Marque, and, while his army slowly passed over it, Philip threw himself down to rest under an ash tree which grew close to a little chapel.

As he lay there a messenger hastened to him, crying that his rearguard had been attacked by Otho, and was in dire need of help. Philip at once ordered a band of soldiers to hasten back to the rearguard. With them he sent the sacred Oriflamme, which had been taken across the bridge before the van of the army. Then the king himself went into the little chapel to pray. Coming out in a few moments he shouted, "Haste we to the rescue of our comrades!" and rode off to meet the enemy "with a glad countenance," while his knights cried lustily, "To arms! to arms!" and followed after their king.

The soldiers of the Communes were the first to attack the knights of Flanders. The knights were indignant that these ill-armed citizens, as they considered them, should dare to oppose them, and they fought desperately, until the French nobles were forced to ride up to the support of the citizen soldiers.

Soon the battle became general, and after three hours' conflict the Count of Flanders was taken prisoner. The German soldiers, remembering their emperor's words, forced their way to the French king, unhorsed him, and all but killed him. Then a great cry arose, and William des Barras, hearing it, let go the German emperor whom he had seized, and sped to the help of his king. The troops of the Communes at the same time rallied around Philip, and he was saved.

Otho's horse meanwhile was wounded. The animal

reared with pain, then turned and fled from the battlefield, carrying his master with him.

The French were now everywhere victorious, and before night the battle of Bouvines had been won.

Many counts were taken prisoners, and these Philip gave to his knights that they might ransom them for a heavy sum of money.

Ferrand, Count of Flanders, however, who had defied the king's summons, was taken by Philip as a prisoner to Paris.

After the battle of Bouvines the French king was, as he had desired to be, the most powerful sovereign, not only in France, but in Europe.

In 1215 King John of England signed the Great Charter, as your English history tells. But he soon annulled it, and then his subjects were so angry that they offered the English crown to King Philip's eldest son Louis.

So Prince Louis went to England, and nearly all the great barons were glad to see him, and flocked to his side. But soon after this King John died, and then the barons were sorry that they had asked a French prince to reign. Now their only wish was to get rid of him, and to make this easier they proclaimed King John's young son Henry, King of England. They then defeated Louis and his French troops at Lincoln, and shut him up in London, where the citizens still supported his cause.

Philip sent a French fleet to aid his son, but it was utterly defeated; whereupon Louis made terms with the English and went back to France, while Henry III. reigned in England.

Besides adding to his dominions Philip improved his capital, and the streets of Paris were no longer allowed to remain narrow or dirty. He also began to build the palace of the Louvre, which was used as a prison as well as a home for the kings of France.

After a long reign of forty-three years Philip Augustus

THE BATTLE OF BOUVINES

died in 1223, having accomplished many of the things he dreamed of doing as a boy.

Of Philip's son, Louis VIII., called the Lion, there is little to tell. He reigned for three years, and during that short time any effort he made for the good of his people was due to the wisdom of his queen, Blanche of Castile.

One of Louis's first acts was to summon Henry III. of England, as a vassal of France, to attend his coronation.

Henry III. was only a child, but the English barons answered that Normandy should be restored to England before their king would own himself a vassal of the French sovereign.

As Louis did not mean to give up Normandy, war was his reply to the haughty English lords.

But after besieging and taking Rochelle, an important town by which the English could easily enter France, Louis made a truce with England, so that he might be free to carry on war against the people in the south of France; for the crusade against the Albigensians had again broken out.

The king led a large army to the town of Avignon, and demanded that he and his soldiers should be allowed to pass, armed, through the city. The citizens refused, and kept their gates shut. Then the king besieged the town, but before it was reduced fever was raging in the French camp.

At length the citizens of Avignon surrendered, whereupon Louis marched away northwards, meaning to return and crush the Albigensians by taking Toulouse.

But the fever which had spread among his soldiers now took hold of the king, and he grew ill and died in 1226.

He left behind him the beautiful and noble Queen Blanche, and a little son of twelve, named Louis.

CHAPTER XX

THE VOW OF ST. LOUIS

"The Hammer," "the Fat," "the Young," "the Wide-awake"—these are some of the names by which the French people called their kings, and they may at times have made you smile.

But now you have come to a king whom his people named "the Saint," and that is a title so great that you will hold in reverence the king to whom it was given. As you read of the reign of Louis ix., you will find that the name became him well.

Louis ix., or St. Louis, lost his father, as you know, when he was only twelve years old. But his mother, Blanche of Castile, trained him so wisely, that when he became a man he was well able to be a king of men.

Blanche taught her son to be kind, unselfish, true, and as soon as he was able to understand, he knew that his mother would rather have him die than that he should say words or do deeds that were unworthy of a king.

The mother of Louis was a brave woman, and she had need of all her courage while her boy was young. For the nobles banded themselves together against the young king and his mother, thinking that now was the time, while the government was in the hands of a woman, to win back the lands and the privileges that had been wrested from them by Philip Augustus.

So when the barons were summoned to Rheims in 1226 to attend the coronation of the little prince, only a few of them obeyed the call. The others assembled an army,

THE VOW OF ST. LOUIS

hoping to subdue the queen and get possession of the young king.

But Blanche was a clever woman, and she determined to win to her side Theobald, Count of Champagne, the leader of the rebel lords. And so successful was she that before long he became her staunch friend. "By my faith, madame," she had the joy of hearing the count say, "my heart, my body, my life and all my lands are at your command, and there is nothing to please you which I would not do, and against you and yours, please God, I will never go." This was a victory for Queen Blanche greater than the victory of a pitched battle.

Two years after he had been crowned the rebel lords still hoped to seize King Louis. For when Blanche had halted with her son at the town of Montlhéry on their way to Paris, she found that the rebel troops were between her and the capital. Undismayed, the queen-mother despatched messengers to the citizens of Paris to ask for help, and right royally did they answer her appeal.

For "they went forth all under arms and took the road to Montlhéry, where they found the king and escorted him to Paris, all in their ranks and in order of battle." Indeed, the road to Paris was lined with men-at-arms, "who besought the Lord that He would grant the king long life and prosperity, and that He would defend him against all his enemies. And this God did."

As Louis grew older, the people learned to love their king, so gentle he was and kind, yet at the same time so brave and strong. Of his love for his people there was no doubt.

When Louis was twenty years old his mother found him a little bride. Her name was Margaret, and she was only twelve years of age.

Good as Queen Blanche was, her love for her son was so great that she forgot that Margaret would sometimes like to be alone with her lord.

Even when the little bride was ill, the queen-mother made so many demands on Louis's time that at length Margaret rebelled, crying indignantly, "Alas, madame, neither dead nor alive will you let me see my lord." After that the king refused to leave the little queen until she was well.

In 1242 Henry III., King of England, came to France with a small army, hoping to win Normandy once again for England. He was joined by Count de la Marche, one of the French king's rebel lords.

But Louis showed the mettle of which he was made. He gathered together a large army, and entering Poitou he took town after town before Henry was ready to fight.

He then marched to Taillebourg on the river Charente. The English, with Count de la Marche, were on the opposite bank, but they had left the bridge across the river unguarded. The French at once began to cross it, and to attack the English. But the enemy was too strong for them, and their ranks began to waver. King Louis, seeing just where he was needed, dashed into the forefront of the fight. The English were forced to give way and retreat to Saintes. Here another battle was fought, and the English were totally defeated. The rebel Count de la Marche surrendered to King Louis, who pardoned him, but kept all the lands which he had won from the Count in battle.

Henry III. fled to Bordeaux, and there he spent his time in pleasure, until in 1243 he made peace with Louis, and returned to England "with as much bravery as if he had conquered France."

But there had been sickness in the French camp, and Louis went back to Paris ill, smitten by the fever which had carried off many of his soldiers.

Day after day the king grew worse, until all over France the people wept, lest they should lose the king they loved so well.

Louis himself believed that he was dying, and said fare-

THE VOW OF ST. LOUIS

well to his household, bidding them be good servants of God.

His wife, his mother, his brothers, lingered in his room, praying that God would spare him whom they loved. But the king lay so still that one of his nurses thought he was dead.

Soon, however, he rallied, and asked to see the Bishop of Paris. When the holy man arrived, Louis, in a feeble voice, begged him to place on his shoulder "the Cross of the voyage over the sea." This could only mean that Louis had made a vow to go as a crusader to the Holy Land.

In vain did Queen Margaret and Queen Blanche entreat the king to make no vow until he was stronger, in vain did the bishop plead with him to wait.

"I will neither eat nor drink," said the king, "until the Cross is laid upon my shoulder." Then the bishop, not daring to refuse, did as the king desired, while his mother, seeing that he had taken the Cross, sorrowed as though her son were dead.

From that day Louis grew better, and there was joy and thanksgiving throughout France.

For three years the king stayed at home, his barons doing all they could to shake his purpose to go to Palestine. But Louis was still determined to go.

The bishop and his mother made one last effort to shake the king's resolve. "My lord king," said the bishop, "bethink you that when you received the Cross you were so weak you scarce knew what you did."

"My son," said the queen-mother, "remember that God loves obedient children." Then, as the king was silent, she added that she would herself send troops to Palestine if he would but stay at home and rule his kingdom.

So quietly did the king listen that for a moment his mother and the bishop believed that they had won the day. Even when he spoke they were not at first undeceived.

"You say that weakness of mind was the cause of my

taking the Cross," said Louis, smiling. "So, then, since you desire it, here I lay down the Cross and resign it to you," and tearing the sign from his shoulder he handed it to the bishop.

Then before either his mother or the holy man could speak, Louis continued, his face grave, his voice firm: "My friends, now I lack not sense and reason, I am neither weak nor wandering of mind. Give me back, then, my Cross. For He who knows all things knows that no food shall pass my lips until my Cross is restored to me."

From that day no one ever again dared to plead with King Louis to give up the crusade.

Some of Louis's knights also took the Cross, but the number was not large enough to content the king, and he determined that many more should follow him to Palestine. If others would not take it of their own will, then they must be persuaded by one means or another.

Grave as King Louis was, I think he must have smiled to himself as he planned to entrap his laggard knights.

It was the custom in those days for each courtier to receive a new cloak at Christmastide. On Christmas Eve, therefore, the king bade them be present next morning at early mass.

As each knight entered the chapel on Christmas morning, his new cloak was thrown around his shoulders by one of the king's officers.

There was nothing unusual in this, and it was only when the service was over, and the knights came out of the dimly lighted chapel into the dawning light of day, that each saw on the new cloak of his neighbor the Cross, the sign of the Holy War.

"At first the knights laughed, seeing that their lord king had taken them piously, preaching by deeds not words," but they soon grew grave, knowing well that they could not tear off the sacred sign which the king had fastened to their cloaks. They must even follow him to the Holy Land.

CHAPTER XXI

ST. LOUIS IS TAKEN PRISONER

In the summer of 1248 Louis unfurled the Oriflamme, gathered together his army, and set sail for the east.

Queen Blanche was to rule the country in her son's absence.

"Most sweet, fair son," she said as she bade him farewell, "fair, tender son, I shall never see thee more, full well my heart assures me." Queen Margaret sailed with Louis, for she had refused to be parted from her dear lord.

When Richard the Lion-hearted left Jerusalem, the city, you remember, was in the hands of the Sultan of Egypt.

It was still in the hands of a Sultan of Egypt, though the one with whom Richard made a truce must long have passed away.

King Louis therefore determined to go, not to Jerusalem, but to Egypt, to attack the sultan where he was strongest. Then after crushing his power in Egypt, he hoped to go on to Palestine.

After spending nearly eight months at Cyprus, and laying in a supply of provisions, the French ships sailed to Damietta, a town at the mouth of the Nile.

In June, 1249, the crusaders at length caught sight of the coast of Egypt. There before them, too, was the town of Damietta. But between them and the town, drawn up on the beach, were the sultan's armies. He had heard that the crusaders were approaching, and he was ready to receive them.

The king was in the foremost ship, from whose prow waved

the Oriflamme. As the boat neared the shore Louis leaped into the sea, though it reached to his shoulder, and holding his shield high in one hand, his lance in the other, he struggled to the shore, followed by his whole army.

Only one ship lay out at sea. In it was Queen Margaret, eagerly watching how the battle would go, anxiously praying that her lord might be safe.

Followed by his army the king dashed upon the sultan's troops, and drove them back upon the town of Damietta. The Saracens were without a leader, for the sultan was ill. A panic seized them and they fled, leaving Damietta with its strong walls and stores of provisions in the hands of the crusaders. Queen Margaret then came with her ladies and her guard to join the king, and to hold her court in the conquered town.

And now Louis, instead of marching on, lingered at Damietta, while the waters of the Nile rose and overflowed its banks, as it does each year. For five weary months it was impossible for the army to leave the town.

While the crusaders were shut up in Damietta, the sultan had recovered from his illness, and was at a town called Mansourah, strengthening the walls of the city against the cruasders.

When the waters of the Nile had gone down, the crusading army at length set out on their march to Cairo, the capital of Egypt. To reach Cairo they must pass the town of Mansourah, where the sultan awaited them.

After a difficult march the army approached the city, only to find that a stream of water separated them from their enemies. Before they could cross they must build a causeway over which to pass and attack the Saracens. But while the crusaders tried to build the causeway, the Saracens were attacking them from the walls and towers of Mansourah, and also sallying out and destroying their work. King Louis saw that it would be impossible ever to finish the causeway. As he gave the order for the soldiers

ST. LOUIS IS TAKEN PRISONER 117

to withdraw from their difficult task, an Egyptian stole into the camp and offered to show the crusaders a ford, if they would give him money as a reward.

The offer was accepted, Robert, Count of Artois, the king's brother, begging to be allowed to pass over first with his men. He promised to guard the ford on the farther side until the whole army had crossed.

But having crossed the ford, the count saw a band of Saracens ready to flee at his approach. At the sight he forgot his promise to guard the ford, stuck spurs to his horse, and, followed by his men, pursued the enemy into the town of Mansourah.

Robert thought the town was his. But he was yet to pay for his rash deed. It was only a small part of the sultan's army that had fled before the count and his followers. The other now came up, surrounded the town, and before Robert was aware, he and his men were fighting for their lives in the place they thought they had taken as easily as they took Damietta.

The king's brother was slain, and three hundred of his knights also perished within the walls of Mansourah.

Meanwhile Louis with the main body of his army had crossed the ford, to find the other bank unguarded by his brother Robert. The enemy fell upon them from every side, while the French army, unable to keep its ranks, fought in small bands. Louis's orders were unheard in the clashing of arms and dire confusion that had overtaken the army. The king himself fought as only a gallant knight could fight, always at the point of danger.

Joinville, a famous chronicler of the times, says, "Never have I seen a knight of so great worth; he towered above all his battle by the head and shoulders."

At one time it seemed that Louis would be taken prisoner. Dashing upon the enemy with only a small bodyguard, in his haste he outstripped his men, and found himself alone in the midst of six fierce Saracens. But Louis did not know what fear meant. He fought so bravely that the six fierce Saracens found it impossible to take him, and before long his bodyguard rode up and rescued their king from his perilous position.

One charge more, one wild determined charge, and the French had won the day, but at terrible cost, for many men were slain, many wounded.

Three days later the Saracens returned in great force, and attacked the king's camp. Again the French were victorious, but there was scarcely a knight that was not wounded, while the numbers of the slain were not to be counted.

Instead of now retreating to Damietta, the king lingered on the battlefield until the army had buried its dead. Meanwhile, fever broke out in the camp, and while the French let the weeks slip by, the enemy watched the river, so that it was wellnigh impossible for Louis to get provisions for his army.

During these sad days the king proved utterly unselfish. No one ever heard him complain, no one ever saw him provide for his own comfort. Though ill himself, he went in and out of the camp among his fever-stricken soldiers, tending them with his own hands, speaking so kindly to them that they were content to die were he but by their side.

One of his own servants, as he lay dying, was heard to murmur, "I am waiting for my lord, our saintly king, to come. I will not depart this life until I have seen him and spoken to him, and then will I die."

After six weeks had passed, the king gave the order to retreat to Damietta. The ships were prepared to receive the sick and wounded, but Louis himself, though now attacked by fever, refused to go on board. "Please God, I will rather die than desert my people," said Louis the Saint, and he placed himself in the rearguard of his army.

ST. LOUIS IS TAKEN PRISONER

The king was too ill to bear the weight of his armor, or to ride his battle-horse, so his servants helped him to mount a little Arab steed covered with silken trappings. The retreat began, but before they had gone far the king grew worse. He could no longer ride the little Arab steed. His knights carried him to an Egyptian house, and sought to guard him from the enemy. But the Saracens burst into the house, and the brave, unselfish king was captured, while the whole army was either slain or taken captive.

Louis was thrown into prison, and from the window he could see his soldiers as they were led out one by one, and asked if they would give up their faith in Christ and become followers of the prophet Mahomet. If they refused they were slain before the eyes of their king, and this to Louis was the hardest part of his captivity.

But he was so fearless, so patient, never flinching even when the sultan threatened to torture him, answering only, "I am your prisoner, you can do with me what you will," that his captor was touched, and offered to give him up on the payment of a heavy ransom. Unselfish as ever, Louis refused to be set free unless the soldiers who still remained in prison were also allowed to return to France.

At length terms were arranged. Damietta was given up as a ransom for the king, an enormous sum of money was paid to the sultan that the French soldiers might also be set free, and a truce was made for ten years.

Then Louis being free went back to Damietta, where Queen Margaret awaited her lord. Her courage alone had kept the soldiers, who held the town, from forsaking their posts when the king was taken prisoner. While the queen had looked with tear-stained eyes for Louis's return a little son was born, whom she named John Tristan, in memory of her sorrow. For Tristan comes from the French word *triste,* which is the same as our word "sad."

The king was now urged by his knights to go home to France, but bidding those return who wished, Louis himself set out for Palestine. Here he labored for four years, setting free the Christians who had been taken captive by the Turks, and strengthening the towns which were still Christian strongholds.

Then, in 1253, Louis heard that his mother, Queen Blanche, had died, and he knew that it was his duty to go home. In September 1254, six years from the time he had set out, the king was once again in his own country. The joy of his people knew no bounds. They lighted bonfires, they danced, they sang in the streets to show their delight, until at length the good king, "who was pained to see the expense, the dances, and the vanities indulged in . . . put a stop to them."

For sixteen years King Louis stayed at home, ruling his realm so wisely that his people loved him more and more. The poor, the sick, the sad, were his special care. Every day, in whatever town the king might be, six score, that is, one hundred and twenty poor people, were fed at his table. And often the good king was to be seen cutting bread, pouring out wine, and himself giving food and drink to the folk who gathered around his palace doors.

But alas! neither Louis's love for his people, nor theirs for him, could keep the king at home. The Cross of the crusader was still fastened to his cloak, nay more, it was branded on his heart.

In the spring of 1270 the king determined to go on another crusade.

Joinville tells us that when Louis set out he was so weak that he was able neither to ride nor walk. The chronicler himself sometimes carried the king in his arms from one place to another, while at other times he was placed in a litter. It was little wonder that the people mourned when they heard of the new crusade. They feared that never more would they see their beloved king.

With his three sons and his army, Louis sailed this time for Africa, landing at Tunis, under the rays of a burning

'THE GOOD KING WAS TO BE SEEN GIVING FOOD AND DRINK TO THE FOLK'

ST. LOUIS IS TAKEN PRISONER 121

sun. Here he halted for reinforcements, which Charles of Anjou, his brother, had promised to bring.

While the crusaders waited, fever and disease attacked the army. The king himself, already weak, was smitten with fever.

In his illness Louis did not forget his people. Calling his eldest son Philip to his side, he said, "Fair son, I pray thee win the love of the people of thy kingdom. For truly I would rather that a Scot should come out of Scotland and rule the people well and justly, than that thou shouldest govern them ill-advisedly."

Then, lying back in bed, he murmured, "Fair Sir God, have mercy on this people that bideth here, and bring them back to their own land."

The day before he died he bade his knights lay him on a bed of ashes, and thus "this most loyal man" passed away.

St. Louis's body was brought to a church in Paris which he himself had built, and his tomb is still to be seen in this church, which is called Saint Chapelle.

Louis was the last of the heroes of the crusades. After his death the Christians were gradually driven out of Palestine, and the land was then left in the hands of the Saracens.

CHAPTER XXII

THE SICILIAN VESPERS

Philip, St. Louis's eldest son, stayed at Tunis for about two months after his father's death. He then made peace with the Turks and set sail for France, taking with him the body of the dead king. From the beginning it was a sad voyage. How could it be otherwise when King Louis was dead?

Before the fleet had been long at sea, a great storm arose and destroyed a large number of the ships. Then Philip's wife, who had been thrown from a horse shortly before, fell ill and died. It was indeed a sad company of crusaders which at length in 1271 reached France.

Philip III. was named the Bold. It is said that he gained the name when he was a child. For one day, seeing his mother, Queen Margaret, shrink back at the sight of some fierce-looking Saracens, the little prince had drawn himself up, saying bravely, "I am not at all afraid." The king would scarcely have been called the Bold from his deeds after he became a man.

King Philip was neither wise nor strong. His uncle, Charles of Anjou, who was restless and ambitious, attracted more interest and attention than his quiet nephew.

While Charles was ruling over Naples and Sicily, and proving himself more powerful than any prince in Italy, Philip was living quietly at home, ruled by his favorite, Peter de la Brosse.

Peter had once been the king's barber, but Philip had made him a noble. The more powerful he became, the more the nobles hated him.

THE SICILIAN VESPERS

The favorite was always to be seen at the king's councils. The barons wished he were anywhere but there, for they knew that if Peter did not approve, their schemes would soon be set aside and forgotten.

The king, you remember, had lost his wife on the way home from Tunis. Four years later Philip had married again, and the new queen, Mary of Brabant, having great influence over the king, did all she could to lessen the power of the favorite, for she hated Peter as much as did the nobles.

Peter, on his side, had no love for the queen. When Philip's eldest son, the queen's step-son, took ill and died, the favorite dared to whisper to the king that Queen Mary had poisoned the prince, that her own child might in time wear the crown of France.

At first the king listened to Peter, but he was soon ashamed that he had done so, for he knew his wife would not do so cruel a deed.

The queen herself did not rest until the favorite was punished. She and the barons watched Peter closely, and at length accused him of treason. After that even the king could not save him. Peter was condemned as a traitor and hanged. The people were not pleased at the fate of the favorite, for he had been one of themselves; but the nobles, so an old chronicler says, "took pleasure in witnessing his execution."

Charles of Anjou, the king's uncle, was, as I told you, King of Naples and Sicily. He was harsh and proud, "neither smiling nor speaking much," and the gay Sicilian people, as well as those who dwelt in Naples, hated their French king and his followers. At length they determined, whenever an opportunity came, to turn Charles and the French out of their country.

Easter, 1282, dawned, while the anger of the Sicilians was still smoldering. The trees were already green, the air warm, as the bells rang that Easter day in the town of Palermo for vespers or evening prayer.

The Sicilians, clad in their holiday gowns, trooped to the service.

Among the crowd were French soldiers, whom Charles had commanded to keep order. But instead of doing their duty, the soldiers behaved so rudely to the people that the Sicilians bade them begone.

"These Sicilians must carry arms or they would not dare to speak so insolently," said the soldiers one to another, and they began to search the peasants. One beautiful maiden they handled so roughly that she fainted. Quick as thought her lover drew his dagger and stabbed the French soldier to the heart.

This was the opportunity for which the Sicilians were waiting. At once a cry arose, "Death, death to the French!" and in a transport of fury the Sicilians fell upon the soldiers, and not one escaped alive. Then the crowd, too maddened with rage to know what it was doing, stormed the houses in Palermo, and killed all who were not Italians.

Throughout the island the rebellion spread, and every Frenchman that was found was put to death. We still shudder as we read of the "Sicilian Vespers," for so the massacre was called, because it began as the vesper bells rang for evening prayer.

When Charles of Anjou, who had been in Naples, heard what had happened, his anger knew no bounds. With a large force he at once set out to punish the Sicilians.

They, knowing themselves defenseless against Charles, offered the crown of Sicily to Pedro, King of Aragon, and begged him to come to their help. Pedro's own kingdom of Aragon was in the north of Spain.

Pedro accepted the crown which the Sicilians offered him, and at once sent ambassadors to Charles bidding him withdraw his troops from Sicily.

In his rage Charles gnawed the top of his scepter; nevertheless, he withdrew to Naples, vowing to return to take vengeance on his foes.

THE SICILIAN VESPERS

Meanwhile, Pedro defeated the French fleet, and took Charles's son prisoner. Rage and sorrow together threw Charles of Anjou into a fever from which he never recovered. He died in 1285.

When Philip the Bold heard that his uncle was dead, he determined to carry on the war with Pedro. He therefore attacked him in his own kingdom of Aragon.

But the town Philip besieged was hard to take, and while the king waited with his army beneath its walls, his fleet, with provisions for the army, was destroyed. His soldiers, too, were already suffering terribly from the heat, so Philip determined to go back to France.

With his army worn out by fever and want of food, it was no easy matter to recross the Pyrenees. As the soldiers struggled homewards, the king heard that the remnant of his fleet had been destroyed. Disappointed and ashamed, Philip fell sick and died before he reached France.

CHAPTER XXIII

THE BATTLE OF THE SPURS

PHILIP the Bold was succeeded in 1285 by his son Philip the Fair. "This king," says an old chronicler, was "simple and sage, and spake but little; proud was he as a lion when he looked on men." But as you read about Philip IV., called the Fair, you will learn more about him than the old writer tells. You will find that Philip was greedy for wealth, greedy for power, and to get either he would do bad and cruel deeds. If he saw that he could not get his own way by force, he was crafty enough to gain it by soft words and pleasant ways.

The king loved money, and Flanders was one of the richest countries in Europe.

Guy de Dampierre, Count of Flanders, was a vassal of the French king. He was a brave man, bent on marrying his daughters to great princes, so that he himself might become of more importance.

When Philip the Fair discovered that Count Guy was secretly trying to arrange with Edward I, King of England, that his daughter Philippa should marry the heir to the English throne, he was very angry. He at once invited Guy to Paris, and the count did not dare to refuse. Being a brave man, Guy, who probably knew why he had been summoned to the capital, no sooner came into the king's presence than he told that his daughter Philippa was soon to marry Prince Edward of England.

As England and France were often at war, the count hastened to add that, in spite of the new tie with England,

THE BATTLE OF THE SPURS 127

he would always serve King Philip loyally, "as every good and true man should serve his lord."

"In God's name, Sir Count," said the angry king, "this thing will never do; you have made alliance with my foe without my wit (knowledge), wherefore you shall abide with me." And without more ado Philip ordered Count Guy and his two sons, who were with him, to be put in the tower of the Louvre. The Louvre, you remember, was a prison as well as a palace.

For six months the king kept his prisoners, and then set them free only on condition that Philippa should stay in France as a hostage for her father's good conduct.

But at the end of two years the count threw off his allegiance to the French king in these bold words: "Every one doth know in how many ways the King of France hath misbehaved toward God and justice. Such is his might and his pride that he doth acknowledge naught above himself, and he hath brought us to the necessity of seeking allies who may be able to defend and protect us."

At the same time Guy made no secret of the treaty he had concluded with Edward 1, by which his daughter Isabel should marry the young English prince, since Philippa was still a prisoner in the Louvre.

After such defiance from the count, it was but natural that Philip should declare war upon Flanders.

A French army was soon assembled, and before the English had arrived to help Count Guy, Philip had marched into Flanders, taken the town of Lille, and won a great victory.

For two years after this there was a truce between the two countries. As soon as it ended, Philip sent his brother Charles, Count of Valois, into Flanders at the head of a powerful army.

When the Count of Valois reached Ghent, however, no battle was fought. For the magistrates came willingly to offer the keys of the city to the French prince.

Perhaps you wonder how the magistrates came to act as traitors to their country.

An old chronicler tells us all about it. "The burghers of the town of Flanders," he writes, "were all bribed by gifts or promises from the King of France, who would never have dared to invade the frontiers had they been faithful to their count."

Guy de Dampierre saw that his cause was lost, and surrendered to the Count de Valois, with his two sons and those knights who had not forsaken him.

Charles urged Guy to go to Paris and trust Philip to be merciful. So Guy set out for the capital, and when he drew near to the palace he dismounted and walked humbly into the king's presence, as befitted one who had come to sue for mercy.

But Philip had no mercy. "I desire no peace with you," he said haughtily, as Count Guy urged his suit, and he sent the count to prison. Then at length he was free to do what for years he had wished. He proclaimed that Guy de Dampierre having forforfeited his right to Flanders, the country now belonged to the crown of France.

In the following year, 1301, Philip thought it would be well to pay a visit to the province he had made his own. So with the queen, her ladies, and a brilliant train of courtiers, Philip the Fair set out for Flanders.

At Bruges the town was brightly decorated to receive the royal visitors. Platforms were placed in the square of the town, hung with rich tapestries. Here the ladies of Bruges were seated, wearing their most precious jewels, their most gorgeous robes.

The Queen of France looked with some displeasure at these richly dressed dames, with some envy at their valuable jewels. Turning to the king she said, "There is none but queens to be seen in Bruges; I had thought that there was none but I had a right to royal state."

But though the rich ladies and nobles were pleased

THE BATTLE OF THE SPURS 129

thus gayly to welcome their new lord, the people would have nothing to do with their conqueror. They refused to put on holiday clothes, to play games, as usually they were quick to do, but went about the streets silent and with sullen faces. Philip had already proved himself a hard master. Not only the inhabitants of Bruges, but the people all over Flanders were beginning to groan under the taxes imposed on them by the King of France.

In March 1302 the Flemings resolved to bear Philip's exactions no longer. Bruges set the example. In the dead of night the bells rang out from every belfry in the town, the burghers rose up as one man, and massacred all the French who were in the city. This was the beginning of a fierce struggle between the French and the Flemings.

The tidings of the massacre no sooner reached Paris than the barons set out with an army to punish the burghers. They met the Flemish force, which had taken up its position behind a deep and narrow canal, near a town called Courtrai, in July 1302.

The French knights feared the burghers of Flanders not at all. Recklessly they dashed forward, putting spurs to their horses so that a cloud of dust enveloped them. On they dashed, the gallant knights of France, nor saw amid the dust the smooth water of the canal. Into the water, before they were aware of it, fell the foremost knights, those behind pressing those in front, until the army was floundering in the muddy water.

Then the Flemish fell upon the French, the rearguard turning to run for their lives. Robert, Count of Artois, the leader of the French army, tried to rally his men in vain. As he fell wounded to the ground he cried, "I yield me! I yield me!" but the Flemish pretended that they did not understand his language, and put him to death.

On the battlefield lay twelve or fifteen thousand soldiers, and among them were the leaders of the French army. The Flemish had won the battle of Courtrai. From the towers of a monastery not far from the town the monks watched the battle. "We could see the French flying," wrote the abbot, "over the roads, across the fields, and through hedges, in such numbers that the sight must have been seen to be believed. There were in the outskirts of our town, and in the neighboring villages, so vast a multitude of knights and men-at-arms tormented with hunger, that it was a matter horrible to see. They gave their arms to get bread."

When all was over, the victors took from the dead bodies of the French knights four thousand or even a greater number of gilt spurs, and hung them as a trophy of war in the cathedral of Courtrai. And ever since this hard-won field has been called the "Battle of the Spurs."

Two years afterwards Philip defeated the Flemish fleet. Then another battle was fought, but both sides claimed the victory. Philip saw that he need never expect to crush these obstinate burghers, so he offered to make peace with them. From that time to the end of his reign treaties were continually being made and broken and remade between France and Flanders.

CHAPTER XXIV

POPE BONIFACE TAKEN PRISONER

You have heard how often the kings of France were at war with the nobles, and how gradually their power was reduced while that of the king increased. Philip IV. struggled, not against the nobles, but against the Church.

Wealthy persons had been used, when they were dying, to leave all their lands and riches to the Church, but Philip forbade them to give her more than a certain portion of their wealth or property. He also refused to let any of the clergy sit in the law courts. Nor was this all. Being in need of money, the king determined that the clergy should be taxed, a thing unheard of until now.

Boniface VIII., who was Pope at this time, was very angry when he heard that the King of France had dared to tax the clergy. He at once wrote to Philip, saying that the priests were his subjects and could not be taxed without his permission. If the king would not "amend these matters of his own good will," the Pope threatened to correct Philip more severely.

Philip could ill brook the Pope's reproof. He answered that the King of France could tax whom he would in his own realm, and had done so before ever a Pope had ruled at Rome.

The Pope with some sharpness retorted that if the king did not humble himself, and that speedily, he, Boniface, would excommunicate him; nay, he would do more, he would even depose him.

As Philip did not submit, a Bull of Excommunication was actually sent to France. The decree was called a Bull from the golden *bulla* or ball to which the Pope's seal was attached. But the bearer of the Bull was thrown into prison when he reached France, and Philip proceeded to attack the Pope.

The French king had in Italy at this time a captain named Nogaret. He, by Philip's orders, joined an Italian prince called Colonna, who for long had had a family feud with the Pope.

Nogaret and Colonna then hired soldiers and set out to seek the Pope, who was staying in a palace in the town of Anagni.

In September the soldiers, led by Nogaret and Colonna, entered the town, the gates being flung wide for them to enter, for Nogaret had bribed the captain of Anagni with gold.

Boniface was an old man, over seventy years of age, but when he heard that his enemies were near, he threw over his shoulders the cloak of St. Peter, put the crown that had belonged to him as Pope upon his head, and, taking the Cross in his hands, awaited the soldiers without a trace of fear. As they entered the palace he said to his enemies, "Here is my neck and here is my head!"

Colonna would fain have killed the old man on the spot, and when Nogaret interfered, the Italian prince is said to have struck Boniface with his mailed hand, until the blood streamed down his face.

The soldiers then sent the Pope's attendants away, placed the old man on a horse, with his face to the tail, and led him away to prison.

For two days Boniface dared neither to eat nor drink, lest his enemies should poison him. On the third day the people of Anagni could no longer bear to think of their Pope in prison. Forgetting their fear of the French, they rose and drove Nogaret's soldiers out of the town,

POPE BONIFACE TAKEN PRISONER 133

and set Pope Boniface free. Then in triumph they led him back to his palace, and because he was faint with fasting, they fed him with bread and gave him wine to drink.

When the Romans heard how the Pope had been treated, they sent their soldiers to bring him back to Rome. But soon after the old man, worn out by all that he had suffered, took ill and died. From that time the worldly power of the Pope was broken.

In the following year, 1304, Philip was forced to recognize the independence of Flanders, and Count Guy's eldest son came to do homage to the French king as his lord. Save for two or three frontier towns, Flanders no longer belonged to the kingdom of France.

The war had emptied Philip's treasury. To fill it Philip did two cruel deeds. The Jews in France were known to be wealthy. The king accused them of horrible crimes, such as using evil spells and poisoning wells of water. Then he banished them from the land, and himself took possession of all their riches.

Not satisfied with this, Philip next attacked the Knights Templar, who were also known to be rich and to possess much property.

Long before this time, in 1119, nine knights had gone to live in a house near the Temple at Jerusalem. They called themselves its Knights Defenders, and were the beginning of the order of the Knights Templar.

At first these knights lived simple lives, under the control of a Grand Master, whose power was supreme. Over their armor the Templars wore a white cloak, with a red cross fastened to it on the left side, over the heart. They were half soldiers, half monks, living on alms, and possessing neither lands nor money, and they were among the bravest of those who fought in the crusades to recover the Holy Sepulcher from the Infidels.

Gradually, when the crusades were ended, the Knights

Templar forgot their vow of poverty. They grew rich and powerful, and owned lands and property in both France and England.

In Paris they built the Temple, which was a strong fortress close to the Louvre, while in London the Temple Church was founded, and took its name from these knights of long ago.

Dark tales began to be told of the order in the reign of Philip IV. People believed that its members trampled and spat on the crucifix. They believed that the knights did many other horrible deeds, and they knew that they were idle and proud.

These tales gave Philip the chance he wished, and in 1307 he suddenly ordered all the Templars in France to be thrown into prison, while he seized their wealth to fill his treasury, just as he had seized the Jews' wealth when he banished them from the country.

Many of the knights were tortured and put to death, while the Grand Master and one other were taken to a little island on the Seine. There, at the hour when the vesper bell called to evening prayer, they were tied to a stake and burned to death.

Philip thought nothing of the sufferings he had inflicted on these knights, but the nation was growing angry with their king's cruelty.

The nobles and burghers leagued themselves together, and presented Philip with a petition, begging him to relax his taxes and oppressions. At the head of those who signed this paper was the name of Joinville, the chronicler of St. Louis's time, who was now almost a hundred years old. Philip was as much surprised as angry when he received the petition. Shortly afterwards, as he was out hunting, he was wounded by a wild boar. From this wound he never recovered, dying in November 1314, at the age of forty-six.

France had suffered too much under Philip's reign to be sorry when she heard of his death.

"God forgive him his sins," says a writer of his day, "for in the time of his reign great loss came to France, and there was small regret for him."

CHAPTER XXV

THE SALIC LAW

Philip iv. left three sons, Louis, Philip, and Charles, who each in turn became king.

Louis x., the new king, was named the Quarrelsome, and though he was twenty-five years old he was neither willing nor able to reign. He left the care of his realm to his uncle, Charles of Valois, while he idled his time playing games or taking part in tournaments.

Charles was an ambitious prince, and the first use he made of his power was to take vengeance on Marigni, a minister of Philip iv., who was sometimes called "the other king," and who had always stood in Charles's way.

One day, when the young king had forsaken his games and was present at a meeting of his council, he asked how, during his father's reign, a certain large sum of money had been spent.

"Sire," answered Charles de Valois, "it is for Marigni to render an account. It was he who had charge of everything."

"I am quite ready," said Marigni.

"This moment then," cried Prince Charles.

"Most willingly, my lord; I gave a portion to you," said Marigni.

"You lie!" shouted Charles.

"Nay, you!" retorted the minister.

Charles, in spite of the presence of the king, was in such a rage that he drew his sword, and Marigni would have unsheathed his, had not other members of the council interfered.

But Marigni, by his rash words, had sealed his fate. Charles de Valois could not rest until his enemy was punished.

The minister was seized, condemned to death without a fair trial, and hanged on a scaffold which he had himself erected. Marigni walked bravely to the place of execution, saying to the people who looked on, "Good folk, pray for me."

King Louis had tried in vain to have the fallen minister's sentence changed into banishment; but the nobles, led by Charles de Valois, paid no heed to the king's wish. Again and again they wrested from the feeble hands of their king privileges and powers which Philip had denied them. At length even Louis x. grew alarmed. He would soon, he felt, be a king only in name.

Yet, in spite of the king's weakness, we find that in 1315 he ordered that all the slaves in the land should be set free on paying a certain sum of money. It was not so much to free the slaves as to procure money that Louis did this, yet it was a great and just act. The slaves, however, had not much money, and what they had they had earned with such difficulty that, rather than part with it, they were willing to remain slaves.

Louis then made a law compelling every slave to buy his freedom, and in this way the money he needed flowed into his treasury. But though the slaves were now free men, the nobles did not cease to oppress them, and it was many long years before they were treated otherwise than as slaves.

War with Flanders had again broken out, and Louis, now having money for a campaign, set out with an army and reached Lys. Here, however, he found that heavy rains had made the roads almost impassable. Food for the army also began to run short, so without more ado Louis returned to France, "not without much inconvenience and some disgrace."

During the last two years of Louis's reign the people of France suffered much from famine and poverty. But the king, caring little for their suffering, played tennis, and forgot all about his starving subjects.

One day as he played Louis became so hot that he slipped away to a cold cellar and "drank wine without stint." This was the cause of the illness from which he died.

Louis, although he had no son to succeed to the throne, left behind him a daughter, named Jeanne. But the king's brother, Philip, paying no heed to the claims of his niece, hastened to Rheims, and was crowned King of France.

When he returned to Paris the new king, Philip v., called the Long, summoned the lords and citizens, and declared to them that no woman could succeed to the French throne.

The lawyers thought that they would strengthen the king's words if they could find in their ancient law books that women had never been allowed to rule in France. So they searched the old law books, and among those belonging to the Salian Franks, from which tribe Clovis, their first king, had sprung, they found what they wished. For in these ancient books they read that "no part or heritage of Salic land can fall to a woman." As a queen must be able to own land, it was plainly impossible for a woman to reign in France. Thus strangely the new law which Philip the Long made to keep his niece Jeanne from seizing the crown was confirmed by the ancient law books. From that time the law forbidding women to rule in France was known as the Salic Law.

In 1322 Philip died, and his younger brother Charles iv., called the Fair, became king.

Philip the Long's children were all girls. It may be that if he had known that he would have no son to follow him he would have been less quick to declare that no woman could rule in France, and the lawyers might never have looked for the old Salian law books. Be that as it may, Philip had prevented any of his four daughters from ever becoming Queen of France.

Charles the Fair was the last of the Capetian kings, for he left no son to carry on his race.

"And thus, in less than thirteen years, perished all the noble and fair lineage of the Fair king, whereat all marveled much; but God knoweth the cause thereof, not me."

CHAPTER XXVI

THE BATTLE OF SLUYS

Two princes now laid claim to the throne. One was Philip, Count of Valois, a cousin of the last three kings; the other was Edward III. of England, whose mother, Isabella, was the daughter of Philip IV. and sister of Charles IV. who had just died.

When the barons and citizens of France met together to choose their new sovereign, they soon determined that Philip of Valois should be their king. For Philip was a Frenchman, while Edward was English; moreover, Philip was a great baron, and the nobles hoped to win his goodwill by raising him to the throne.

In this, however, they were doomed to disappointment, for Philip proved ungrateful and cruel. No sooner was he crowned than he began to put down the nobles, whose power he feared might clash with his own. For though Philip was called king, he owned no more land and possessed little more power than some of his subjects.

The new king, Philip VI., was called the Fortunate, which seems strange, for his reign was full of misfortunes.

Being fond of show, Philip was crowned with more than usual magnificence at Rheims, and for many days after the coronation the court was gay with dances and tournaments.

The merriment of the court was, however, interrupted by his cousin Count Louis of Flanders, who begged the king to come to his help, for the Flemings had rebelled against him.

THE BATTLE OF SLUYS

Philip, thinking a fine army and the glory of winning battles a better entertainment than were the gayeties of the court, readily promised to give Louis his help.

It was easy to raise an army, for the barons were eager to conquer and plunder the obstinate burghers of Flanders, who were known to be wealthy.

So "with the fairest and greatest host in the world," Philip VI. marched into Flanders and encamped at the foot of a hill called Cassel.

The Flemings had encamped on the top of the hill, and were eager to fight. Their captain, however, wished first to find out the strength of the enemy. Disguising himself as a fish merchant, he clambered down the hill and boldly entered the French camp. While selling his goods he saw that the French knights had taken off their armor, and were playing at chess or "strolling from tent to tent in their fine robes, in search of amusement," while the king was sitting at supper, as undisturbed as though he were in the midst of his gay court at Paris.

As quickly as he dared the fish merchant made his way out of the French camp, and hastening back to the Flemings, told them that now was the time to take the French by surprise.

Almost at once three columns of soldiers crept silently down the hill, and attacked the French camp, Philip himself being nearly captured.

In spite of their surprise the French quickly rallied, and fought so bravely that the Flemish captain as well as most of his men were slain.

This defeat ended the rebellion in Flanders. The Flemings submitted to Count Louis, and Philip disbanded his army and returned in triumph to Paris.

The king was proud of his success, and perhaps it was partly in pride that he now summoned Edward III. of England to come to do homage to him for the duchy of Guienne.

Edward came with his barons, and met Philip and his peers in the church of Amiens.

Froissart, a chronicler who tells us much about these days, says that Edward did homage to Philip "only with mouth and word," refusing to put his hands into the hands of the French king, as was the custom at such a ceremony. By so doing Edward believed he left himself free to claim the crown of France.

Philip, guessing that Edward hoped some day to put forward his claim to the French crown, set himself to harass his rival in every possible way.

He did all he could to spoil the English trade with Flanders; he attempted to take from the English king his duchy of Guienne; and, when Edward went to war with Scotland, he helped and encouraged Robert the Bruce to defy his rival.

Edward had little time to think of Philip until his war with Scotland was ended. Then he determined to punish the French king for the injuries he had done him by laying claim to the crown of France.

This, then, was the beginning of the long struggle between France and England known as the Hundred Years' War, because it lasted all those years, with, however, times of peace in between.

In 1337 Edward III. declared war against the French king; the Flemings, encouraged by Jacob van Artevelde, a rich brewer, being his allies. Three years later the first great battle of the Hundred Years' War took place at sea, the French fleet being near the seaport of Sluys, a town in Flanders. Before this the fleet had cruised from time to time in the Channel, and sailed into English ports. One Sunday morning, while the people were at church, the French had even sailed up to Southampton, and sacked and burned the town.

Then at length, in June 1340, Edward was ready to avenge this and other hostile acts. He sailed from London

THE BATTLE OF SLUYS

with a large fleet, on board of which were England's bravest soldiers.

As they drew near to Sluys the English saw the masts of the French fleet, so many in number that they looked "thick as a forest before them." The *Christopher*, too, their own English ship which the French had captured a year before, was there. You can imagine how angry the English soldiers and sailors felt when they saw their own good vessel in the van or front of the enemy's fleet. They made up their minds that, at all costs, they would again gain possession of the *Christopher*.

Edward was well pleased when he saw his foes. "For many a long day," said he, "I desired to fight those fellows, and now we will fight them, please God and St. George."

The sun was shining directly upon the English fleet as it approached Sluys. Edward, seeing this, ordered the sails to be lowered and the ships to be turned so that the sun would be behind them.

The French watched the great ships as they changed their position, and soon they cried, "They are turning tail, they are not men enough to fight us." But in that they were mistaken. For the English bore down upon them, and, grappling their ships together with hooks and chains, fought on deck with their battle-axes and swords as though they were on land.

You may be sure that the English did not forget to attack the *Christopher,* and before long it was taken, manned once again with English archers, and working deadly havoc among the French.

The battle was fierce and long, lasting from eight in the morning until five in the afternoon. As the day wore on the French were pushed back upon Sluys, and there the Flemings fell upon them; and many thousands, some say thirty thousand, were slain, or, jumping into the sea to save themselves from the enemy, were drowned.

By afternoon the great sea-battle was over, and the English had won the day.

Philip was at Paris when tidings from Sluys reached the capital. But no one dared to tell the king how the day had gone. Yet he must be told.

At length the court fool, a jester who might say what he pleased, cried out, "The English are great cowards."

"Why do you say so?" asked the king.

"Because they lacked courage to jump into the sea at Sluys as the French did," answered the fool.

There was no need to say more. Philip understood that the English had beaten him, and his anger was terrible. Even the fool was quick to flee from his master's presence.

Soon after this great defeat a truce was arranged between France and England, and King Edward went back to his own country.

CHAPTER XXVII

THE BATTLE OF CRÉCY

In July 1346, the truce being over, King Edward sailed for Normandy, taking with him a large army and his eldest son, the Prince of Wales.

Having landed, Edward marched through the country, taking town after town. St. Cloud, the town named, you remember, after a hapless little prince, was burned, and the English troops advanced almost to the gates of Paris.

Philip at once prepared to join his army at St. Denis. The old blind King of Bohemia had come with his son Charles and his knights to help the French king, and was awaiting him there, as was also a band of archers from Italy, who had been paid to fight for the French army.

The citizens of Paris were alarmed by the approach of Edward's troops, and begged the king not to leave them.

"My good people," answered Philip, "have ye no fear; the English shall come no nigher to you; I am away to St. Denis to my men-at-arms, for I mean to ride against these English and fight them in such fashion as I may."

So Philip joined his troops and set out in pursuit of the English, who had now turned northwards and were marching toward the river Somme. The French were about a day's journey behind, but they hoped to overtake them at the river, for they knew that Philip had ordered all the bridges to be either broken down or fortified.

When Edward heard from his captains that it was impossible for the army to cross the river, he was, says Froissart the chronicler, "not more joyous or less pensive, and began to fall into a great melancholy." For well he knew that the enemy was not far behind.

But Philip was triumphant. He believed that the English were already in his power. He would starve them there between the river and the sea, or force them to fight against his army, which was larger and stronger than theirs.

Just when the English were most despondent, however, a ford was discovered. For King Edward had himself sent for some French prisoners, promising them freedom and gold if they would tell him a spot where the army might safely cross the river.

And one prisoner proved a traitor, for he led the English to the point where the Somme enters the sea. Here at low tide it was easy to cross, so the English bestirred themselves, and as the tide was ebbing they plunged into the water.

Guarding the opposite bank, by Philip's orders, was a knight, Sir Godemars de Foy, with about twelve thousand men. They also leaped into the river, and meeting the English in the middle of the stream they did their utmost to bar the passage. Many, both French and English, were drowned or slain.

But the English archers, from the farther side, never ceased to speed their arrows among the enemy, until at length the French began to yield, and, in spite of all Sir Godemars could do, to turn and run. They were pursued by the English, who overtook and scattered them, and thus Edward and his army were soon safe on the other side of the river.

By this time the tide had again begun to rise, and Philip, coming up, found it impossible to follow the enemy, though his men killed some of the rearguard who had lingered behind.

Edward now marched on until he reached a small village called Crécy. Here, on rising ground, on August 26, **1346**, the army took up its position.

THE BATTLE OF CRÉCY

The English were in three divisions. In the van or forefront was the king's young son, the Prince of Wales, who was only seventeen years of age. As the armor he wore was always black, he was called the Black Prince. On the field of Crécy the young prince was to win his spurs.

King Edward, having divided his army, mounted upon a pony, and with a white staff in his hand he rode from rank to rank, bidding his men fight bravely for the honor of their country.

Froissart tells us that some of the soldiers were sad because the French army was so much larger than their own. But the presence of the king so cheered them that those who "had before been disheartened felt reheartened on seeing and hearing him."

When the king had reviewed the whole army he gave orders that the men should be given food. So, sitting down on the ground, the soldiers ate their morning meal, and rested until the French should arrive.

Meanwhile, Philip's army was on its way, its ranks all in disorder. The king commanded four knights to ride forward to find out what the enemy was doing.

They soon returned to tell how the English, rested and refreshed, awaited them on the summit of a little hill. Looking at the straggling ranks of their own men, they then advised Philip to halt and let the soldiers rest and have food. "For the English," they said, "are cool and fresh, and our men are tired and in disorder."

So Philip commanded his marshals to call a halt. They at once rode along the ranks, crying, "Halt banners, by command of the king, in the name of God and St. Denis!"

At the cry the soldiers in front halted, but those behind still pressed forward, wishing to be the first to see the enemy.

When the soldiers in front saw that if they stood still they would lose their position, they too began to march on, heedless of the order of their king.

Before they were aware they were close to the English;

and, taken by surprise, the van of the army halted, while those behind still pressed forward, until the French army was little more than a pushing, struggling mob of men.

King Edward, with some men-at-arms, had withdrawn to a windmill which stood on the hillock, whence he could see the unbroken ranks of his own men and the confusion in the ranks of the French.

"They are ours," cried the men-at-arms, before ever the battle had begun.

Philip, seeing the English whom he hated, no longer wished to delay the battle, and he cried aloud to the hired archers, "Archers, begin the battle, in the name of God and St. Denis!"

But the archers were tired, and had expected to rest before they fought. Their bows, too, were slack, and they were in no mood to obey the king's orders.

While they hesitated a sudden storm broke upon the army. Thunder roared, lightning flashed, while rain fell in torrents, wetting the strings of the foreign archers. But the English kept their crossbows dry beneath their coats. It was only a passing storm, and soon the sun shone out, blinding the eyes of the French army.

Then at length the hired Italian archers unwillingly advanced, shouting and singing, thinking thus to frighten the English. But they paid no heed to the foreign soldiers' cries.

The Italians drew their bows. In a moment the sturdy archers of England had taken one step forward, and sent their arrows among the enemy. So sharp and fleet they sped that "it looked like a fall of snow."

Never had the Italians felt such stinging arrows. They were everywhere, around them, above them, beneath them. It was impossible to escape from these terrible darts.

At length, in despair, they flung down their bows and turned to flee.

Philip saw them throw their bows away, and in terrible

THE BATTLE OF CRÉCY

anger he bade the French soldiers kill the cowards. As the soldiers obeyed, the English arrows still sped swift, unerring, until Italian archers and French soldiers fell together in a confused mass.

Meanwhile, on another part of the field, the Black Prince was being hard pressed by the French. Though he was fearless and fought gallantly, the English knights were anxious lest the prince should be slain.

So they sent a messenger to the king to beg him send more men to the aid of his son.

Edward, watching from the windmill as the battle raged ever more fiercely, asked:

"Is my son dead or unhorsed, or so wounded that he cannot help himself?"

"Not so, my lord, please God," answered the messenger, "but he is fighting against great odds, and is like to have need of your help."

"Then return to those who sent you," said the king, "and tell them not to send for me, whatever chance befall them, so long as my son is alive; and tell them that I bid them let the lad win his spurs; for I wish, if God so deem, that the day should be his."

When the old blind King of Bohemia heard that the battle was going against the French, he asked his knights, "Where is my son Charles?"

But they would not break the old king's heart by telling him that his son had fled from the battlefield. Instead they lied, saying that Charles was doubtless fighting in another part of the field.

Then the blind king begged his knights to lead him to the front of the field, that he too might strike a blow for victory.

So the knights gathered up their horses' reins, and tied themselves together that they might not be separated. Then placing the king before them they rushed into the fray "like madmen bent upon sudden death." But before death came the blind King of Bohemia had "struck a good blow, yea three and four, and so did all those who were with him."

When the battle of Crécy was over, the blind King was found dead, while his knights and their horses still tied together lay slain beside him.

Philip fought bravely, but his heart was heavy, for he knew the day was lost. It was nightfall when he rode away from the battlefield, attended by only four barons. When they reached the Castle of Broye they halted. It was dark and late and the castle gates were shut, the bridge drawn up.

"Who knocks?" cried the castellan from the tower, as the fugitives roused him by their thundering knocks.

"Open, castellan!" said Philip. "It is the unhappy King of France."

Then the keeper of the castle hastened down, lowered the drawbridge, and opened the gates to the king and his barons. After refreshing themselves with wine they set out again at midnight, and before dawn entered Amiens, where the king stayed until what was left of the French army reached him there.

CHAPTER XXVIII

THE SIEGE OF CALAIS

After the battle of Crécy Edward with his victorious army marched to Calais, and laid siege to the town. Calais was on the coast, and would be a safe and convenient haven for the English when they wished to sail to France.

It was in September 1346 that King Edward arrived at Calais. He knew that the town was too strong to be taken by assault, but he believed that if he could starve its inhabitants they would be forced to surrender.

So the king prepared for a long siege, building around Calais another town, made of wood, in which he determined to live, summer and winter, until Calais was taken.

The governor of the besieged town was John de Vienne. He soon saw that even with great care the food in the city would not last long. So he ordered the old men, women and children, who could not fight, to leave the town.

One day the sad procession passed slowly out of the gates of Calais, and came to the English town.

The English soldiers asked them why they had left the city. "We are poor," they answered, "and are either too old or too young to fight, so the governor has sent us away, for he cannot feed us during the siege."

When King Edward heard what had befallen these hapless folk, he ordered that they should be given a good dinner. After their meal they were allowed to go away, the king first giving a two-shilling piece to each of the forlorn band, "the which grace," says Froissart, "was commended as very handsome, and so indeed it was."

Winter passed, spring came, and then summer, and during all these months Philip had sent no help to Calais. Famine stared the defenders of the city in the face. Sometimes fisher folk in the neighborhood had succeeded in getting food into the town, but even this had now ceased to be possible.

John de Vienne wrote in despair to King Philip, "Everything has been eaten, cats, dogs, and horses, and we can no longer find victuals in the town, unless we eat human flesh.

"If we have not speedy succor, we will issue forth from the town to fight, whether to live or die, for we would rather die honarbly in the field than eat one another."

At length, in July 1347, Philip with a large army was seen to be approaching. How the starving folk rejoiced when they saw the banners of their king floating in the breeze. Now their hunger would soon be satisfied, now the gates of Calais would soon be flung wide open, and once again they would be free.

But day after day passed, and Philip could find no way to reach the town, so well were all its approaches guarded by the English king. Each day seemed a year to the starving people, yet their hopes were still centered on the king. But alas! while Philip talked of peace he found no way to reach the starving folk.

It had been some comfort to the people to crowd upon the walls of Calais, and look at the tents of Philip's army, where there was food in abundance, food that soon would surely be theirs. But one day in August, to the dismay of the starving folk, they saw that the tents were gone. Philip and his army were marching away from the besieged town. Then indeed the brave inhabitants of Calais were in despair. Their last hope was gone. Their king had not fought a battle to save them; nay, he had not even managed to send them a little food; he had gone away and left them to their fate. Sobs and cries broke from the hearts of the desperate, starving people.

THE SIEGE OF CALAIS

There was now nothing to be done but to submit to the King of England, and Sir John de Vienne tried to make terms with the victor.

But Edward was in no mood to make terms. The siege had lasted long, and the king had lost many brave soldiers and spent much good money while the citizens of Calais had held their city against him.

He sent Sir Walter de Manny to the governor of the town to say that it must be surrendered to him without any conditions, while the inhabitants were to yield themselves to him that he might do with them as he would.

"The terms are too hard," pleaded John de Vienne to Sir Walter. "Go back and beg your king to have mercy upon us."

So Sir Walter went back to King Edward, and besought him to grant easier terms to the brave men of Calais.

At first the king refused to listen, but when all his knights added their entreaties to those of Sir Walter, the king at length yielded.

"Go then," he said, "and tell the governor of Calais that the greatest grace they can find in my sight is that six of the most notable burghers come forth from their town bare-headed, bare-footed, with ropes round their necks, and with the keys of the town of Calais in their hands. With these will I do according to my will, and the rest I will receive to mercy."

John de Vienne listened until Sir Walter de Manny had delivered his message, then slowly he went to the market-place, and bade that the great bell of the city be rung. As the clang of the bell, slow and solemn, fell upon the ears of the people, they hastened to the square to hear what their brave governor had to tell.

But when they knew the king's will, the poor starving folk wept bitterly. Even John de Vienne could no longer try to comfort them, for the tears were streaming down his own cheeks as he saw the despair of the people.

Bitterly the hungry folk wept, for they deemed that there was not one, and certainly that there were not six, burghers who would give their lives to save them all from death.

Then, so Froissart tells us, as the sobs of the people fell upon his heart, Eustace de St. Pierre, the richest burgher of the town, arose.

"Sir," he said to the governor, "it would be a great pity to leave this people to die by famine or otherwise. . . . I have great hope to find favor in the eyes of our Lord if I die to save this people."

When the people heard these words they threw themselves at the feet of the good man, weeping for joy. Then slowly, one after another, five other burghers stepped forward, and offered to give up their lives for the sake of the other citizens of Calais.

On the 5th August 1347 St. Pierre with five burghers noble as himself, bare-headed, bare-footed, with ropes round their necks, and the city keys in their hands, walked along the streets of Calais, followed by the tears and blessings of the starving folk they were leaving behind.

When they reached the gates they were thrown open, and the six burghers passed bravely out to their doom.

As King Edward gazed upon these men in their pitiful guise, he grew angry, remembering his own good soldiers who had perished during the long siege, and he ordered that the six burghers should at once be beheaded.

The king's knights begged him to be merciful, but Edward only bade them be silent and do his will.

Sir Walter de Manny dared yet again to plead that the burghers' lives might be spared. "Gentle sir," he said to the king, "you have renown for gentleness and nobleness, be pleased to do nought whereby it may be diminished."

But the king turned upon the knight furiously, saying, "Sir Walter, hold your peace. Let them fetch my headsman."

Then his wife, Queen Philippa, fell at her lord's feet. "Ah, gentle sir," she cried, "I pray you humbly, as a special boon, for the sake of Holy Mary's Son and for the love of me, you will please to have mercy on these six men."

As he looked at the queen bending at his feet, the king's heart at last grew kind, and he answered, "Ha, dame, I had much rather you had been elsewhere than here. But you pray me such prayers that I dare not refuse you, and though it irks me to do so, there, I give them up to you; do with them as you will."

Gladly Queen Philippa thanked her lord. Then rising to her feet she speedily led the six burghers to her own rooms. Here they were clothed in clean robes and given a good dinner, for well the queen knew that for many months they had had nought to eat save only enough to keep them alive. Then the brave burghers were sent safely back to the people for whom they had dared so much.

Calais now belonged to the English, and for more than two hundred years it remained an English stronghold.

Philip had suffered heavy losses during the war, and in 1347, when the siege of Calais was over, he was glad to agree to a truce with England for ten years.

Thus, for a time, France was delivered from war. But a terrible calamity, as bad as war itself, overtook her in 1348, for the plague called the Black Death, which had already been causing havoc in Italy, reached France.

Men, women and children were stricken down in a day by the dread disease. And there were few who dared to tend the sick, lest they too should catch the terrible illness. Only a few monks and nuns went bravely in and out among the dying people, carrying with them for protection nought save the Cross of Christ.

For two long years the Black Death claimed its victims. Then, in 1350, it gradually disappeared, and men, women and children were able once again to do their work, to play their games, without fear clutching at their hearts lest they should be the next to be smitten with the Black Death.

While the Black Death still raged, the lord of Dauphiny,

chastened it may be by fear of the terrible plague, determined to go into a monastery. He therefore sold his land to Philip, on condition that it should never be joined to the crown of France, but should always belong to the eldest son of the king. From this time, therefore, the eldest son of the French king always bore the title of the Dauphin, and ruled over the land which had once belonged to the lord of Dauphiny.

Philip, like other kings of whom you have read, was often in need of money, and to procure it he had put heavy taxes on his subjects. Before his death he imposed a new tax on salt, called *Gabelle*. This tax was bitterly resented by the poor people both now and in later years.

In 1350 Philip the Fortunate died. And you have seen for yourselves that never was a less fitting name found for any king than the one the people bestowed on Philip of Valois.

CHAPTER XXIX

THE BATTLE OF POITIERS

Philip's son John now became king. He was named "the Good" by his favorites, not because they thought their king was an upright, noble man, but because they knew him to be a "good fellow," who loaded them with gifts.

King John was rash, cruel, and selfish, yet he was also brave and chivalrous, when to be so did not interfere too greatly with his pleasures.

Charles the Bad of Navarre was a kinsman of John the Good, but for all that the king hated him, and wished to make war upon him. For John had had a favorite to whom he gave lands, which Charles of Navarre claimed as his. In his anger that the king had thrust aside his claims, Charles the Bad had killed the king's favorite. It was for this crime that John was determined to punish his kinsman.

But Charles was supported by many of the lords of France, as well as by the friendship of the King of England. It was therefore impossible for John to war against Navarre without being forced to fight with England as well, and for this France was not yet ready.

King John therefore pretended to forgive Charles, who was also, I should tell you, the king's son-in-law. He even received him at court, when Charles the Bad thanked him for his grace on bended knee.

But those who knew him best felt sure that King John had not really forgiven Charles. They had heard him mutter, "I will have no master in France but myself. I shall have no joy as long as he is living."

John's son, Charles the Dauphin, was at this time made Duke of Normandy. He became good friends with Charles the Bad, and in the spring of 1356 he asked him, with some of his friends, to a banquet at Rouen.

The party was a merry one, but the merriment was suddenly disturbed by the entrance of King John with a troop of soldiers, and an officer who held in his hand a naked sword.

"Let none stir, whatever he may see, unless he wish to fall by this sword!" said the officer in a loud voice.

King John meanwhile moved toward the table, and the dauphin and his guests rose to greet their sovereign. But the king paid no attention to any one save Charles the Bad.

Drawing him aside, he said, "Get up, traitor, thou art not worthy to sit at my son's table. By my father's soul, I cannot think of meat or drink so long as thou art living." Then King John bade his soldiers take Charles of Navarre prisoner.

The dauphin flung himself at his father's feet, and begged him not to harm his guests. "It will be said that I have betrayed them," he cried in distress.

But the king thrust his son aside, and ordered the barons who had come with Charles the Bad to the feast to be beheaded.

Charles himself John sent to prison, where he was kept in constant fear as to what was to be his fate. For each day his guards told him that, at a certain hour, he would be beheaded, and when the hour had passed and Charles was still alive, they told him another hour at which he would be thrown into the river Seine.

As you may imagine, a king who could treat his son's guests so treacherously, and who could torture his prisoner in the way Charles the Bad was tortured, was not likely to be loved by his people. More and more his subjects grew to hate him, and some of his barons deserted King John and served in the army of the King of England.

THE BATTLE OF POITIERS

After the siege of Calais a truce, you remember, was made with England for ten years. Nine years had passed, but, though no great battle had been fought during that time, the truce between the two countries had not been strictly kept. King John had even made an attempt to get back Calais, but had failed. Now, however, in 1356 the Black Prince had landed in France at Bordeaux, and leading his army northward into the country of the river Loire, he had burned and pillaged the towns through which he passed.

When King John heard of the Black Prince's march, he at once set out with a large army, hoping to be able to cut off his return to Bordeaux. For the Black Prince, knowing that the French army was much larger than his own, was now on his way back to the coast, so that, if it were necessary, he might embark for England.

But King John succeeded, as he had hoped to do, in coming between the prince and Bordeaux, near the town of Poitiers.

Then, because the French army was many times larger than his own, the Black Prince offered to give up all the towns and castles he had taken, to set free all the French prisoners, and to promise not to fight against France for seven years, if he and his army were allowed to march on unhindered.

King John would not accept the offer of the prince. He was determined to give battle to the English, unless the Black Prince and all his army would give themselves up to him as prisoners.

To this the English prince never dreamed of agreeing. Then King John said he would be content with the Black Prince and one hundred of his knights.

But to this demand also the prince refused to listen, and preparing for battle, said fearlessly, "God will defend the right."

If its numbers were small, the position of the English

army was good. For it had taken its stand upon a rough hillside covered with vineyards. To reach the hill from the front there was but one way, and this was through a narrow lane, on either side of which was a thick hedge. Behind these hedges the Black Prince had placed his archers, who were thus unseen by the French.

At the foot of the hill lay John's large army. Had the French been willing to wait, they could have guarded every approach to the hill and starved the English into submission. But they were eager at once to win the victory, which they never doubted would be theirs.

As John moved among his soldiers he was surrounded by nineteen knights, each wearing the same dress as the king, so that he might be less easily recognized in the battle. Before the knights waved the Oriflamme from St. Denis.

The vanguard of the French army was now ordered to advance. Up the narrow lane the soldiers rode, when to their astonishment they were greeted on either side by a shower of arrows from an unseen foe. And the deadly shower never ceased, for the English archers poured their darts upon the miserable soldiers so fast, so sure, that they worked deadly havoc. The lane was soon filled with the slain and wounded.

Those who were behind, seeing how their comrades were being smitten, turned backward upon the men who were led by the dauphin.

At the same moment the English archers broke from their hiding-place behind the hedges, and dashed upon the retreating foe.

The Black Prince seized the same moment to ride down upon the enemy, shouting, "St. George! St. George!" and soon the French were flying in every direction.

Among those who fled was Charles the Dauphin, with two of his brothers, followed by about eight hundred knights.

But King John was no coward, and soon he had rallied

THE BATTLE OF POITIERS

his men and prepared to make a stand against the English, who had come down from the hill and held no better position than the French.

The Black Prince, Froissart tells us, "who aimed at perfectness of honor, rode onward to meet the French, with his banner before him, succouring the people whenever he saw them scattering or unsteady, and proving himself a right good knight."

In the midst of his knights King John fought as bravely as the Black Prince, defending himself with a battle-ax. By his side was his young son Philip, a lad of fourteen, who tried his best to ward off the blows that were aimed at his father.

And ever above the strife his clear young voice rang out, "Father, strike here; father, strike there." It was on the field of Poitiers that Philip earned his name "the Bold," which was his when he became the Duke of Burgundy.

"Yield you, yield you, or else you die!" cried the English, as they hurled their blows at King John, some not knowing that it was the king, others knowing it well.

The Oriflamme fell to the ground as the knight who guarded it was slain, and then at length King John and his brave son Philip were taken prisoners and led before the Black Prince, who received them courteously, "as he well knew how to do," says his chronicler.

In the evening, when the battle was ended, the Black Prince asked King John, his son, and many of his noble prisoners, to supper. Nor would the prince sit at table with his royal captives, even when King John begged him to do so, but he himself waited on his guests at though they were his lords.

It was not a merry supper party, and King John looked so sad that the Black Prince, kneeling before him, said, "Dear sir, be pleased not to put on so sad a countenance, because it hath not pleased God that you should win the day, for the prize of valor is yours, since every Englishman saw that none bore himself as bravely as you."

Some time after he had won the battle of Poitiers, which was fought on the 15th September 1356, the Black Prince sailed for England, taking with him his royal prisoner, King John.

When they reached London, the Black Prince and his captive rode through the streets of the capital, and while the people cheered their gallant prince, they marveled to see him riding on a little black palfrey, while his prisoner was mounted on a noble white steed. But this was one of the ways which the brave prince took to show King John that he would treat him royally and well. King Edward, too, was kind to the great captive his son had brought home; nevertheless, King John was kept a prisoner in England for four years.

CHAPTER XXX

THE REBELLION OF JACQUES

DURING the four years that King John was kept in England, Charles the Dauphin, who had fled from the field of Poitiers, ruled over France in his father's stead. But the country was in a miserable state, and Charles was too young to govern it with the strong hand which it needed.

Hired soldiers, called Free Lances, who fought for whoever paid them the largest sums, wandered through the country. And the people of France learned to dread and hate these Free Lances, who showed respect to none, and who robbed and killed all who came in their way.

The nobles, too, treated the peasants worse than slaves, until at length they forsook their miserable huts, and went away into the forests to live in caves. For no hardships were so great as those which their masters laid upon them.

It seemed to the nobles that the peasants would always suffer without a word, and they mocked at their sullen faces, and nicknamed them *Jacques Bonhomme,* or as we would say, "Jack Goodfellow."

But the barons made a mistake when they thought that the peasants would submit to their exactions for ever.

For at length, in 1358, goaded into desperation by the cruelty of their lords, the peasants armed themselves with scythes and pitchforks, or any weapon on which they could lay their hands, and attacked the nobles, burning their castles, slaying their wives, and even their little children. Then they wandered through the country, the poor peasant women dressed in the fine garments they had stripped off the wives of the nobles.

This revolt of the peasants was called the *Jacquerie,* or the Rebellion of Jacques, from the name *Jacques Bonhomme,* given so carelessly by the barons to the peasants on whom they trampled. Other risings of the peasants in after-years were also called by the same name.

At first the nobles were alarmed at the fury of the *Jacquerie.* Charles the Bad, who had been set free when King John was taken prisoner, invited the leaders of the rebellious peasants to meet him, pretending that he wished to help them. But when they came he cruelly put them to death, first placing on the head of their chief a red-hot iron. Only then did the nobles take courage to go out against the *Jacquerie,* and hunt them to death as they would have hunted wild beasts.

Meanwhile, in Paris itself there was great unrest. Etienne Marcel, the chief magistrate of the city, demanded that the dauphin should reduce the heavy taxes which King John had laid on the people.

Charles paid no attention to Marcel's demands, so the magistrate, with a band of armed men, forced his way into the dauphin's presence as the prince talked with his two chief advisers, the Counts of Champagne and Normandy.

The armed men wore caps of red and blue, which colors were worn by the rebellious citizens.

Marcel no sooner saw Charles than he boldly demanded that the taxes should be reduced. The Counts dared to interrupt the magistrate, whereupon Marcel turned to his fellows with the red and blue caps, saying sternly, "Do that for which ye are come."

In a moment the rough citizens had seized the Counts of Champagne and Normandy, and slain them in the presence of the dauphin. He, thinking that he also would be slain, fell at Marcel's feet, miserably begging for mercy.

"Take no heed, lord duke," said the magistrate, "you

THE REBELLION OF JACQUES

have nought to fear," and he placed his own red-and-blue cap on the dauphin's head.

But though Marcel saved the dauphin's life, Charles never forgave him for the death of the counts.

Some time later the citizens of Paris grew jealous of Marcel's power. They asked the dauphin, who had fled from Paris, to return. But he refused to do so while Marcel was alive in the city.

Marcel, knowing that his influence over the citizens was fast passing away, turned to Charles of Navarre, promising him the keys of the capital if he would come to his help against the dauphin and the people of Paris.

Charles would gladly be master of Paris. His ambition whispered to him that it was but a step from being master of Paris to becoming King of France, and he accepted Marcel's offer with eagerness. On a certain night, therefore, he came with his followers to one of the gates of Paris to receive from Marcel's hands the keys of the city.

But there was a traitor among Marcel's friends. The citizens learned what the magistrate had promised to do, and as he went at midnight, with a few of his followers, to seize the gates and open them to Charles of Navarre, a troop of citizens fell upon him and put him to death. They then sent for the dauphin, who came back in triumph to the city.

King John all this time was still a prisoner in England. The French now wished to set their king free, but King Edward's terms were so hard that the dauphin refused to agree to them.

Edward therefore determined again to make war on France, and win in battle the towns the dauphin refused to give to him as the price of his father's freedom. Early in 1360 he landed at Calais with a large army, and marched through France, burning and plundering the country, which was already miserable enough with its own quarrels and rebellions.

At length King Edward encamped before Paris, where Charles the Dauphin, or the Regent as he had now been called for some time, was watching his progress.

But the English army was not strong enough to attack the city, and the Regent had no intention of leaving the safety of its walls to risk a battle.

So King Edward, finding it difficult to provide food for his army, withdrew from Paris, and in May 1360 agreed to make peace with France.

By the Peace of Bretigny, Edward III. gave up his claim to the French throne, keeping however many of his French provinces. King John was also set free, his son, Louis of Anjou, promising to remain at Calais as hostage until the king's heavy ransom was paid.

The people of France rejoiced when the Treaty of Bretigny became known, for they were tired of the cruel war, and longed for peace.

And King John returned gladly to his own country, his long captivity at an end. But before a year had passed, Louis of Anjou, who had promised to stay in Calais as hostage until his father's ransom was paid, broke his word, and escaped from the city.

King John, who in spite of his many faults would not have broken his plighted word, upbraided his son, saying that, "If good faith were banished from the world, it ought to find an asylum in the hearts of kings."

The king showed that his displeasure was real, for he himself went back to England to "make the excuses of his son, the Duke of Anjou, who had returned to France."

For a short time King John was once again a prisoner, but three months after his return to England he took ill, and died in April 1364.

CHAPTER XXXI

SIR BERTRAND DU GUESCLIN

CHARLES V., named the Wise, you have already known as the Dauphin who fled from the field of Poitiers, and who begged on his knees that the magistrate Marcel would spare his life. But Charles the Dauphin and Charles the Wise were two very different persons.

The king was tall and thin, and looked so sad that his subjects had no great love for him. His health was so poor that they seldom saw him. As for the nobles, they loved their sports and their tournaments, and paid little attention to their melancholy-looking king.

But before long the nation awoke to the fact that a strong, wise hand was ruling France. The hand belonged to Charles V., who spent most of his time in a quiet room in one of his palaces.

Unlike the kings who came before him, Charles was not able to lead his armies to battle. It was therefore necessary that he should have a good general.

And Charles was fortunate, for in Bertrand du Guesclin, a knight of Brittany, he found one of the bravest and strongest leaders of men.

"Bertrand du Guesclin," says a chronicler of the time, "was the ugliest child in the district in which he lived. As he grew up he became broad-shouldered, big-headed, always ready to strike on being struck."

Guesclin became one of the Free Lances of whom I have told you, and led Free Lances like himself to battle. But though the hero of Brittany was a rough and cruel soldier, to the poor, to women and children, he was ever kind and gentle.

Until he was thirty Guesclin was little known, either for his strength or his goodness, save amongst the knights of Brittany. But Charles the Wise had heard of Sir Bertrand, and when in 1364 he became king, he sent one of his marshals to the knight, to engage him to fight on behalf of the King of France.

Their first exploit, for the marshal and Guesclin fought side by side, was to take a town belonging to Charles the Bad, King of Navarre. Their next was to dash into another town with their wild Free Lances, shouting "Death, death to all Navarrese!" This town they also took, "whereat Charles v. was very joyous when he heard the news, and the King of Navarre was very wroth."

As was but natural, Charles of Navarre was eager to avenge these wrongs. He assembled a large army of Free Lances, and put them under a famous officer called the Captal de Buch.

Guesclin also collected a strong force from Brittany, and from the bands of Free Lances that were eager to serve under so great a captain as Sir Bertrand.

As the two armies drew near to one another, Guesclin disclosed his plan to his comrades.

"The Captal," he said, "is, as you know, a gallant knight. Until he is taken he will do us great hurt. Therefore let thirty of our boldest pay heed to nothing, but make straight toward the Captal, take him captive, and lead him away from the field, without waiting for the end of the battle."

Guesclin's comrades agreed that the plan was a good one. "The picked thirty, well mounted on the flower of steeds, and with no thought but for their enterprise, came all compact together to where was the Captal, who was fighting right valiantly with his ax, and was dealing blows so mighty that none durst come nigh him; but the thirty broke through the press by dint of their horses, made right

SIR BERTRAND DU GUESCLIN

up to him, halted hard by him, took him and shut him in amongst them by force. Then they bore him away, whilst his men, who were like to go mad, shouted, 'A rescue for the Captal! a rescue!' But nought could avail them or help them, and the Captal was carried off and placed in safety."

After a desperate struggle the Captal's banner was then captured, torn to pieces, and trampled underfoot. Guesclin and his men had won the day.

Charles v. was so pleased with his general that he made him Marshal of Normandy, on condition that he should clear the land of the bands of Free Lances that still wandered all over the country. But this condition Guesclin, being himself a Free Lance, took little trouble to fulfill.

In his next battle the knight was taken prisoner by the English. But Charles v. could not do without his general, and willingly paid a heavy ransom that Sir Bertrand might be free.

Then in 1367 Guesclin was sent into Spain to fight against Pedro the Cruel, who oppressed his subjects and had even slain his own wife.

At first he was successful in this war, but when Pedro was joined by the English under the Black Prince, Guesclin was defeated and again taken prisoner.

Before long, however, the knight was set free, and this is the story of how it happened.

One day, being in a merry mood, the Black Prince began to talk to Sir Bertrand.

"My lords counsel me not to set you free," said the prince to his prisoner, "not so long as there is war between France and England."

"Sir," answered Guesclin, "then am I the most honored knight in the world, for they say in the kingdom of France and elsewhere that you are more afraid of me than any others."

"Think you, then, that it is for your prowess that we keep you?" said the prince, his gay mood changing to a haughty one. "Nay, by St. George, fix your own ransom and you shall be free."

Guesclin named so large a sum that the prince was surprised.

"Sir," said Sir Bertrand, seeing his astonishment, "the king, in whose keeping is France, will lend me what I lack; and there is not a spinning-wench in France who would not spin to gain for me what is necessary to put me out of your clutches."

The brave prisoner was then set free to collect his ransom, giving his word of honor to return to captivity if he could not find the money.

But he succeeded in getting the sum that was necessary, and, so the story goes, was riding cheerily on his way back to the Black Prince, when he met ten sad and weary-looking knights, who had been trying in vain to find money for their ransoms.

Then Sir Bertrand, with ungrudging heart and open hands, gave to these sad knights all the money which he had painfully gathered together for his own freedom, and himself went back into captivity. It was for deeds such as this that Sir Bertrand du Guesclin was beloved by all who knew him. The good knight's captivity lasted but a short time longer, for the King of France himself paid his knight's ransom.

Meanwhile the Black Prince, whose constant wars had made him ill and irritable, had levied such heavy taxes on his subjects in Aquitaine, that they appealed to Charles v. to help them.

The king was pleased to quarrel with the Black Prince, for he had been watching for a chance to make war upon England, and here was the opportunity he had wished. He summoned the prince to Paris to defend himself against the complaints of his subjects in Aquitaine, and bade him come as quickly as he could.

When the Black Prince heard Charles's message he

answered after a moment's silence, "We will go willingly at our own time, since the King of France doth bid us, but it shall be with our helmet upon our head and sixty thousand men at our back."

Perhaps the king had expected some such answer from so gallant a knight as the Black Prince, and since it meant war with England, Charles was content. He at once sent for Guesclin and made him Constable of France, Constable being the title of the Commander-in-chief of the French army.

Guesclin was dismayed at so great an honor, and begged the king to bestow this office and title upon one of higher rank. "For," said the sturdy knight, "how can I lay commands on those who may be relatives of the king himself?"

"Sir Bertrand, Sir Bertrand," answered the king, "do not excuse yourself after this fashion. I have no brother, nor cousin, nor nephew, nor count, nor baron in my kingdom, who would not obey you; and if any should do otherwise, he would anger me so that he would hear of it. Take therefore the office with a good heart, I beseech you." So Guesclin became Constable of France.

It was in April 1369 that war once more broke out between France and England. But the hold of the English on France had grown slighter during the years that Charles the Wise had been ruling, and it was now the more easily shaken off.

In the war that followed the French were everywhere victorious. The Black Prince was too ill to lead his men so well as he had been used to do. Indeed, sometimes he was so weak that he had to be carried on a litter to the battlefield.

Meanwhile the constable marched across France, taking towns that had long been held by the English, driving out English garrisons, and everywhere making terms favorable to the French king.

Following the advice of Charles the Wise, Guesclin took

care not to risk a battle with the enemy. So the Black Prince, seeing that the French were safe in strongly fortified towns, led his army to Bordeaux, and set sail for England.

By this war the English had lost all their large possessions in France, being left with only Bordeaux and a few towns in Normandy.

King Edward was now an old man, yet wishing to win back what he had lost, he raised an army and sailed from Southampton. But it was autumn, the gales were fierce, and for nine weeks the king struggled in vain to reach the French coast. At length, in despair, he gave orders to make again for the English shore.

"Never was there King of France," he said, "who wore so little armor, yet never was there one who has given me so much to do."

In 1375 a truce was again made between France and England. The following year the Black Prince, who had long suffered from fever, passed away; while in 1377, the year that the truce with France ended, Edward III., who had been sorely grieved at the loss of his son, also died.

Charles v. now determined to join Brittany to the crown of France, but the Bretons, led by their Lord, John de Montfort, rose in rebellion. The king ordered Guesclin to go to punish them. But the constable, you remember, was himself a Breton, and he ventured to advise the king to make peace with Sir John de Montfort.

This led to a quarrel between Charles and his faithful servant. Guesclin, angry with the king, sent the sword which he wore as constable back to his master, which was as if he had said, "I will no longer be commander of your army."

But the king, who cared for no other, cared for Guesclin, and refused to let his constable go. Instead of being sent to Brittany, Guesclin was ordered, in July 1380, to go to

SIR BERTRAND DU GUESCLIN

the south of France to besiege a fortress still held by the English.

After the siege had lasted some time, the governor of the little town promised to give up the keys of the fortress to the constable if help did not reach him before a certain day. Before the day came Guesclin took ill. His captains gathered around his bed as he lay dying; and the constable, who had seen rough deeds done in his day, said to them, "Captains, never forget, in whatsoever country you are making war, that churchmen, women, children, and the poor people, are not your enemies." Then he passed away.

It is said that when the governor of the town heard that the constable was dead, he begged still to be allowed to put the keys of the town into the hands of the commander.

So, marching out of the fortress at the head of his men, the governor was led to the tent where Sir Bertrand lay. Then, sobbing the while, he laid the keys in the still hands of the great soldier.

There was great sorrow at the death of Guesclin. "Let all know," says the chronicler, "that there was there no knight, nor squire, French or English, who showed not great mourning."

As for the king, he ordered that the constable should be buried in a tomb near to one which had been built for himself.

Nine years later, the son of Charles v. ordered a second funeral service to be held at the tomb of Sir Bertrand du Guesclin, the hero of Brittany, the king himself, with his lords and barons, being at the ceremony.

A poet who was also there wrote some verses on the hero. Here are a few of the lines which you may like to read:

> "The tears of princes fell,
>   What time the Bishop said,
> 'Sir Bertrand loved ye well,
>   Weep, warriors, for the dead.

> "'The knell of sorrow tolls,
> For deeds that were so bright,
> God save all Christian souls,
> And his—the gallant knight.'"

Two months after the death of Sir Bertrand, in September 1380, Charles v. fell ill and died. It was said that he had been poisoned by his enemy, Charles the Bad, King of Navarre. Soon after this the King of Navarre himself was burned to death by an accident.

CHAPTER XXXII

THE BATTLE OF ROOSEBEK

CHARLES THE WISE was anxious that his little son should be well trained for his kingly duties.

Before his death he had sent for two of his brothers, the Duke of Berri and the Duke of Burgundy, as well as for his queen's brother, the Duke of Bourbon.

To them he entrusted the little prince, saying, "Behave to him as good uncles, and counsel him loyally in all his affairs. All my trust is in you; the child is young and fickle-minded, and great need there is he should be governed by good teaching."

For the Duke of Anjou, his other brother, the king had not sent, because he knew him to be selfish, greedy, ambitious, and unfit to take charge of his little nephew.

If the little prince was fond of excitement and games, it was only natural, and he had simple, boylike tastes. Shortly before his death Charles v. told his son that he might choose any one of his most beautiful jewels. The boy glanced at the sparkling stones, then passed them by and chose instead a little helmet. Beside the helmet he hung at the top of his bed a tiny suit of armor, too small to wear, but which seemed to give great pleasure to the little prince.

While the boy-king was young, his four uncles ruled his kingdom. They were called the "Princes of the Lilies," because on their shields they bore the royal arms of France, gold lilies or *fleur-de-lys* on a background of blue.

There are different legends told about the *fleur-de-lys.*

Far back, in the time of the Merovingian kings, the royal banner was blue with gold lilies. At first it is supposed the emblem was meant to represent the head of a javelin, or it may have arisen from the custom among the Franks of placing a "reed or flag in blossom," instead of a scepter, in the hands of each newly crowned king. In the Middle Ages the *fleur-de-lys* was the emblem of the Virgin Mary. It was also often to be seen in church banners and altar decorations. In 1789, as you shall hear, the beautiful banners of the *fleur-de-lys* were replaced by flags of blue, white and red, called the Tricolor.

The Duke of Anjou was one of the "Lily Princes." He was very angry that Charles v. had not summoned him to the royal bedchamber along with his brothers. But though the dying king did not know it, the duke had hidden himself in the next room, and the moment his brother had breathed his last he seized the crown jewels, and all the gold and silver he could find. He then asked the treasurer to tell him where the king had concealed the rest of his wealth.

The treasurer made an effort to be true to his dead master, and said that he had promised not to tell. Without a moment's hesitation the Duke of Anjou ordered the faithful servant to be beheaded.

But the man's faithfulness could not stand so severe a test, and he hastily told the duke where he would find the king's secret treasure.

It was this greedy duke who was now made regent. But he had no wish to stay at home and govern France, for his heart was set on becoming King of Naples. So he raised an army to march into Italy to fight for the crown he longed to wear.

But he could not leave France as soon as he wished, for although he had seized the treasures of Charles v., the duke had not enough money to pay his soldiers, so he laid heavy taxes on the citizens of Paris.

THE BATTLE OF ROOSEBEK 177

The townsfolk refused to be taxed to pay for the duke's foreign wars. Arming themselves with clubs or any weapon they could seize, they killed those who came to collect the taxes. Then working themselves up into a frenzy, the mob broke open the prisons, and set free the prisoners to join in the riot.

Even the greedy duke saw that he must abolish his taxes if he wished to quell the revolt before more harm was done. So he promised to reduce the taxes, and the citizens, trusting to his word, laid down their arms.

No sooner had they done so than the duke ordered the leaders of the riot to be arrested. Then, in the dead of night, he made his soldiers tie them up in sacks and throw them into the river Seine. The cruel duke then went away with his army to Italy.

But misfortune dogged his steps. Before he had been long in Italy food began to run short, and it was impossible to buy provisions, for the King of Naples took care that none should be sent to the prince who had come to take his crown.

The duke offered all he possessed for food, but in vain. His anger and want of proper nourishment left him an easy prey to fever, which now attacked him, and from which he never recovered.

Philip, Duke of Burgundy, then became regent. This was the Philip who fought so bravely by his father's side at the battle of Poitiers.

Almost at once he was forced to march into Flanders to put down a rebellion of the burghers against the Count of Flanders.

The burghers were led by Philip van Artevelde, a son of the great brewer who had helped Edward III. at the battle of Sluys.

When the burghers heard that the Duke of Burgundy, with the young king and an army, was coming to punish them for their rebellion, they were dismayed, for the English had refused to come to their help.

Philip van Artevelde, however, assembled his captains, and bade them have no fear, for they were defending the liberties of their country.

"Tell your men," he said, "to show no quarter. We must spare the King of France only; he is a child, and must be pardoned. We will take him away to Ghent and have him taught Flemish."

Meanwhile, the Duke of Burgundy, who had reached Flanders, had given the young king into the charge of Oliver Clisson, who had been made constable after the death of Guesclin.

Clisson knew it was an honor to have charge of the little king, but he also knew that his soldiers would need him in the midst of the battlefield. He therefore begged Charles to excuse him.

The boy-king answered, "Constable, I would fain have you in my company to-day. You know well that my father loved and trusted you more than any other. In the name of God and St. Denis, do whatever you think best." So Clisson went back to his soldiers.

At Roosebek, not far from Courtrai, where you remember the Flemings had won a great victory, another battle was now fought in 1382.

Philip van Artevelde, seeing the numbers of the French, began to lose a little of the great confidence he had had, while the French insolently said, "These fellows are ours; our very varlets might beat them."

The Flemings, however, fought bravely, tying themselves together so as to advance in a solid body upon the enemy.

But Clisson was a good general, and soon he had surrounded the burghers, and was attacking them on every side. It was impossible for the burghers to escape, and even had they been able they would probably have been too proud to flee from the field. Thus almost the whole

THE BATTLE OF ROOSEBEK 179

army of Ghent perished, while the leader of the rebellion, Philip van Artevelde, was also slain.

As the Flemings now again submitted to their count, the French were soon able to march home. Charles was proud of his first victory. He himself took the Oriflamme, which had been at the head of the army, back to St. Denis, and the following day he marched with his army into Paris.

The loyal citizens came out, as was their custom, to welcome their king, to rejoice in his victory. But Charles and the Duke of Burgundy refused their homage, and curtly bade them begone. For the citizens had rebelled against the heavy taxes imposed on them by the regent, and the king, urged by his uncles, now resolved to punish them.

Perhaps the victory at Roosebek had made the king eager to use his power. In any case, more than three hundred of the principal citizens were, in 1382, put to death by his order.

Among these was one named Jean des Marests, a clever lawyer, who had often during the last two years made peace between the regent and the people. But he had also advised the citizens to carry arms and put up barricades for the defense of the city when the regent had increased the taxes.

Jean was condemned to death, in spite of all his good offices. On the way to the place of execution he was put on a car "higher than the rest, that he might be better seen by everybody." He was seventy years old, yet when he heard his cruel sentence he remained undisturbed, saying only, "Let them come and set forth the reasons for my death."

When Jean reached the place of execution, the people cried, "Ask the king's mercy, Master Jean, that he may pardon your offenses."

Des Marests, when he heard the people's words, answered, "I served well and loyally his great-grandfather, King Philip, his grandfather, King John, and his father, Charles. None of these kings had anything to reproach me with, and this one would not reproach me any the more if he were of a grown man's age and experience. I don't suppose that he is a whit to blame for such a sentence, and I have no cause to cry him mercy. To God alone must I cry for mercy, and I pray Him to forgive my sins."

When the citizens had been duly punished, the taxes, especially the hated salt tax called the *Gabelle*, were again imposed.

CHAPTER XXXIII

THE MAD KING

IN the summer of 1385 Charles VI., who was not sixteen years of age, married Isabelle of Bavaria, a selfish and cruel princess.

Three years later the king began to rule his kingdom himself, dismissing his uncles from the court, yet thanking them graciously for the trouble they had taken to rule the realm. Their nephew's kind words did not soothe the Lily Princes, who were very angry with the king for sending them away.

His uncles being gone, Charles recalled many of the old ministers who had served his father. But the king's greatest trust was in the Constable Clisson, whom he both loved and admired.

For a time the new government pleased the people, for justice was restored and taxes were lowered. This change lasted only for a short time, for Charles was fond of feast and tournament, and he spent such enormous sums on his amusements that the treasury was soon empty, and once again the taxes had to be raised.

But the king loved war as well as amusements. He began to collect an army to fight against England, and at the same time he ordered a wooden town to be built. This town he intended to carry to England, and set up as a fortress upon her shore.

When his fleet at length set sail, it got no farther than two miles out to sea, for a storm arose and drove it back. As no one save the king had much faith in the expedition, it was not again attempted. But before the orders to unload the fleet and place it in a safe port had been carried out, the English sailed down upon the French, taking many of their ships and the provisions stored up in them. Thus even the king was forced to give up his hope of invading England.

All this time the king's uncles were nursing their anger at the government being taken out of their hands. They hated the constable, as well as the king's other advisers, many of whom were of humble birth. These the Lily Princes, in their scorn, called *Marmousets,* which means "Monkeys."

It is said that they did more than give those they disliked nicknames. But whether or no it was the doing of the dukes, it is certain that one night Clisson was attacked in the streets of Paris, and wellnigh killed.

Charles, who, as I told you, loved the constable, was very angry when he heard what had happened. He was preparing for bed when tidings of the attack reached the palace, and the king at once insisted on going to see the wounded man.

Clisson was faint but conscious when the king reached him. He whispered to Charles that it was a servant belonging to his brother, the Duke of Orleans, who had attacked him.

The king at once determined to punish the assassin, who had fled to the Duke of Brittany for protection. If the assassin were not given up he would make war on Brittany.

In August, 1392, the king therefore set out for the duke's domains with an army. His uncles were with him, although they had no wish to see the assassin given up to justice.

Charles himself was not well. He had had fever, and his physicians had forbidden him to go out in the hot days of August.

Nevertheless, the king would go. He was dressed in a tight velvet jacket, while on his head he wore a scarlet cap, adorned with pearls. His clothing was not suited for the heat, which was intense.

Behind Charles rode two pages, the army being some distance off, so that the dust they raised as they marched might not reach the king.

Just as Charles entered a thick forest, a tall man, dressed in a white smock, with bare head and bare feet, dashed out from behind a tree, and, seizing the king's horse by the bridle, cried, "Go no farther! Thou art betrayed!"

The king was startled, as well he might be, by this strange, wild-looking man, yet he determined to go on.

As the heat grew more intense, one of the pages fell half asleep as he rode slowly along behind the king. Suddenly the lance he carried slipped from his grasp, and fell with a crash against the helmet of the other page.

Charles started, and looked wildly around him. Then, drawing his sword, he set spurs to his horse and dashed forward, crying, "Treason! treason!" He then turned furiously upon his pages, chasing them backwards and forwards. His uncles and lords, hearing the king's voice, hastened up, but before Charles could be secured he had killed four of his escort.

The heat and the fight had made the poor king mad. His people carried him home, and at first his physicians thought that he was dead, so quiet and still he lay. But after a time his body grew strong again, although his mind was never again really well, save for some few short intervals.

Sometimes, usually in spring, the poor king's madness having passed away, he would try to do some good to his people, to put some wrong right. And his subjects, full of compassion for the misery of their king, called him Charles the Well-beloved, and wished that he would live for ever.

But again and again his brain grew weary, and he was forced to leave his kingdom and his people to the care of his uncles, the Lily Princes. Yet for thirty long years, from 1392 until 1422, the crown of France still rested upon the head of the poor mad King Charles VI.

Isabelle, the king's wife, cared nothing for Charles's suffering, and left him alone to the care of his attendants, by whom he was for a time terribly neglected. His children, too, took no notice of their father.

But Valentina, the beautiful Duchess of Orleans, his brother's wife, was always kind to the poor king, who called her "his fair sister," and was always a little happier on the days that he saw her.

Sometimes the king was able to be amused by a game of cards. The game was little known in France at this time, though Philip of Valois had learned it in his day. The play, where the scenes were usually taken from Bible stories, also interested Charles. These sacred plays were called "Mystery Plays."

At first the Dukes of Burgundy and Berri were sorry for their nephew. And, indeed, to see him was a piteous sight. But soon they could not help being glad that they would once again be able to govern France.

They put aside the claim of the king's brother, the Duke of Orleans, and made themselves regents of the kingdom. Often they would persuade the poor mad king to sign measures which they wished to become law, but which Charles, had he known what he was doing, would never have signed.

Yet the people never lost their trust in their king. They continued to call him the Well-beloved, and believed that were he but able to rule, justice would again be done in the land.

CHAPTER XXXIV

THE TWO LILY PRINCES

During the next ten years France was ruled by the Dukes of Burgundy and Berri.

The Lily Princes wished to remain at peace with England, so they encouraged Richard II, son of the Black Prince, to ask for the hand of little Isabelle, the daughter of Charles VI.

Isabelle was only ten years old, but she was a wise little princess, who early learned to speak with courtly ease. The English ambassador, who had come to France on his master's behalf, kneeling before the child, said, "Madame, please God you shall be our sovereign lady and Queen of England."

Whereupon the maiden answered, "If it please God and my lord and father that I should be Queen of England, I would be willingly, for I have certainly been told that I should then be a great lady."

In March 1396 Richard II. and Isabelle were married, and a truce was then signed which was to last for twenty-eight years. But three years later King Richard was deposed, and Henry Bolingbroke then became Henry IV. of England. Isabelle was sent back to France.

Ten years passed, and then Charles VI., being a little better, determined that his brother the Duke of Orleans should become regent, as was his right. But Orleans taxed the people so heavily that they turned to the Duke of Burgundy, who loved France, and cared for the rights of the citizens. Orleans was forced to retire. Even the king, when he was well, agreed that after all it was better that his uncle should again become regent. From this time, however, the Duke of Burgundy and his nephew, the Duke of Orleans, were rivals and hated one another.

Unhappily, soon after this, Philip, Duke of Burgundy, died, and his son John the Fearless became duke. John hated Louis of Orleans even more than his father had done, and was determined to become regent in his stead.

At first the Duke of Orleans proved so much more powerful than John the Fearless that John was persuaded to make peace with his rival. But it was not a real peace, though the two dukes swore to be friends, heard Mass, and took the Sacrament together in November, 1409.

Before the winter was over, John, Duke of Burgundy, broke his vow of friendship, and that in a most treacherous manner.

For one evening the Duke of Orleans, after having dined with Queen Isabelle, was riding home, attended only by two squires and a few servants carrying torches, when suddenly eighteen or twenty armed men rushed out of an alley in which they had been hiding, and attacked the duke, shouting, "Death! death!"

Haughty and indignant, Louis demanded what was the matter. Then, thinking that his name would cow the rough fellows, who had probably mistaken him for an enemy of their own, he said, "I am the Duke of Orleans."

"It is he whom we seek," was the unexpected answer, and in a moment the ruffians had struck the duke to the ground and slain him.

The Duke of Burgundy did not hide that the terrible deed had been done by his order. After confessing it to the Duke of Berri, he mounted his horse and, leaving Paris behind him, rode off unhindered to Burgundy.

But he did not stay there long. If he had ridden away for safety, he soon found he had nothing to fear in the capital. The citizens of Paris, who had hated the Duke

THE TWO LILY PRINCES 187

of Orleans, were glad that he could trouble them no more; while for the Duke of Burgundy who had slain him, they had nothing but gratitude. Even the poor mad king said he was not angry with John the Fearless for murdering his brother, but perhaps he hardly knew what he was saying.

There was only one who really mourned the death of the Duke of Orleans, and that was his beautiful wife, Valentina, the lady who was always kind to the poor weak king.

She threw herself weeping at the feet of Charles, and demanded that her husband's murderer should be punished. The king wept with his "fair sister," but he had no power to help her.

Meanwhile, the Duke of Burgundy came back to Paris, and with him were a thousand men-at-arms. The people greeted him with joy, shouting lustily, "Long live the Duke of Burgundy!"

Being sure of the people, the duke, so confident he was, then wrote his own pardon, and easily persuaded King Charles to sign it. Charles even received him kindly, but warned the duke to guard himself against those who would never forgive his crime. To which the duke proudly answered, that "as long as he stood in the king's good graces he did not fear any man living."

There was certainly nothing to fear either from the king or the people. But Queen Isabelle had always been on good terms with the Duke of Orleans, and the duke determined to win her favor. In this, too, he was successful, and through the queen's goodwill he gained possession of Charles, the young dauphin.

But John the Fearless had an enemy, and that a determined one. This was the son of the man whom he had killed, Charles, the young Duke of Orleans.

Charles had married the daughter of Bernard of Armagnac, a count who had great power in the south of

France. He, along with the Duke of Berri and other nobles, joined the Duke of Orleans in his struggle against John the Fearless.

As the Count of Armagnac was the leader of the Orleans party, those who followed him were called "Armagnacs." First one party was in power and then the other, and for many years the story of France is the story of the cruel deeds done by the Burgundians and the Armagnacs.

At length, in 1414, things began to go badly with the Duke of Burgundy. His followers were driven out of Paris, and even out of their own provinces, while the duke himself fled into Flanders, where he was forced to make terms with the Armagnacs.

The dauphin meanwhile was at Paris, enjoying himself too well to give heed to the quarrels of the nobles, and behaving as though he were already king.

CHAPTER XXXV

THE BATTLE OF AGINCOURT

Edward III., King of England, had, as you remember, conquered a large part of France. Before his death, however, many of the towns and provinces he had won were retaken by the French, while during the reigns of Richard II. and Henry IV. England lost all that was left of her possessions in France save Calais.

Henry V., who in 1413 became King of England, determined to win back these French possessions.

He disliked the dauphin, who, shortly after Henry had become king, had sent him a present of tennis balls, with a message that it would be well for him to stay at home and amuse himself with these, rather than seek to win a kingdom in France. Henry also knew that France was so weakened by the quarrels of her nobles among themselves, that she had little strength to resist a foreign foe.

The King of England therefore sent to France to ask for the hand of Catherine, daughter of Charles VI., and to demand as her dowry the three important provinces of Normandy, Maine, and Anjou, as well as a large sum of money. Henry intended, if his demand was granted, to keep peace with France; if it was not granted, he meant to declare war. But crushed as the French were by the struggles of their nobles, they were not so crushed as to agree to Henry's proposals. The king therefore proclaimed war against France, and in August 1415 he sailed up the Seine and landed at Harfleur, which he at once besieged.

For five weeks the town held out, thinking each day

that the royal army, which was now commanded by the Constable d'Albret, would come to its aid. But as no help came, the town was forced to surrender to the English, who themselves were more worn out by the siege than the French suspected. Many of Henry's soldiers had indeed gone back to England ill, many more had died from fever, while those who were left were in no fit state to fight.

Henry, however, would neither stay in Harfleur nor return to England. With his army, which was now a small one, he made up his mind to march through Normandy, as English kings had done before. When he reached Calais he would take his soldiers back to England.

So the men set out on their dreary march, and each day they became more tired and weak, for it was impossible to get food. The French had burned all the farms in the district, and carried off all the stores of food and wine that they could find. Yet tired and hungry as they were, the English struggled on, wet to the skin by the heavy rains of autumn, for it was already the month of October. The country through which they marched seemed utterly deserted; not a sign of the French army was to be seen.

But the French had been roused by the fall of Harfleur, and they had assembled a large army, nearly five times as large as the English.

Charles VI., who was less mad than usual, wished to march with his army, but the Duke of Berri would allow neither the king nor the dauphin to be on the battlefield.

"Better lose the battle," he said, "than lose the battle and the king." For the duke had been at the battle of Poitiers in 1356, and remembered how on that terrible day King John had been taken prisoner.

Meanwhile, Henry was within forty miles of Calais, having only once caught sight of the French in the distance. Now, on October 24, 1415, he found that the army in all its strength had taken up its position between him

THE BATTLE OF AGINCOURT

and Calais. It was plain that, tired and hungry as the English were, a battle would have to be fought before they could reach their haven.

The constable sent a messenger to the English king to ask him when, and at what place, he would be willing to engage in battle. Henry v., regardless of the miserable state of his army, sent back a defiant answer.

"Tell your master," said the king to the constable's messenger, "I do not shut myself up in walled towns. I shall be found at any time and anywhere ready to fight if any attempt is made to cut off my march."

On October 25, 1415, the battle accordingly took place, near the little village of Agincourt.

The evening before the battle the French created five hundred new knights. These spent the long hours until dawn on horseback, in their heavy armor, while the rain fell in torrents, soaking the ground around them. In the morning the new-made knights were as tired as though they had already fought a battle.

As the rain beat down upon the English camp, the soldiers rolled up the banners to keep them dry, the archers carefully put new cords to their bows, while stakes were driven into the marshy ground to check the first attack of the French cavalry. Then the soldiers confessed their sins, and after praying to God, lay down to rest on beds of straw. Not a sound was heard in the English camp, for the king had ordered silence. A knight if he disobeyed would lose his horse, a soldier his right ear.

With the dawn the English could see the great numbers of the French army, and one knight said to another, "It were well if we had ten thousand archers from merry England with us to-day." "Nay," said the king, who had heard the knight's words, "I would not have one more. It is God who hath appointed our number." While to the officer who came to tell him the exact number of the foe, Henry with his indomitable spirit answered only, "There are enough to be killed, enough to be taken prisoners, and enough to flee."

As the day grew light, the French cavalry was ordered to attack the English archers. They dashed forward bravely, but their horses soon stuck fast in the muddy ground. Making desperate efforts to struggle on, the poor beasts but sunk the deeper in the mire. And all the while the English archers were pouring in upon them an unceasing shower of arrows.

At length a portion of the French cavalry reached the enemy's lines, only to find their horses driven upon the stakes which had been fixed in the ground by the English soldiers.

Wounded by the stakes, pierced by the arrows, the frightened animals turned and plunged madly back among the French foot-soldiers, throwing them into utter confusion.

Then down upon the surging mass of wounded men and frightened beasts came the English, armed with axes, clubs, swords. At the sight a panic overtook the French army, and in complete dismay all who could fled from the field.

Never did a more complete defeat overtake the French than on the field of Agincourt. Little quarter was given, yet the number of prisoners was great. As the battle drew to a close, a report spread that the Duke of Brittany, with a large force, had come to the help of the French.

King Henry, fearing that his prisoners would be in the way, then gave orders that these hapless, unarmed soldiers should at once be killed. And this cruel order has ever been a blot upon the fair fame of Henry v., King of England.

On the battlefield lay slain, their banners by their sides, many of the nobles of France. The constable also had perished, while among the prisoners of high birth were the Duke of Orleans and the Duke of Bourbon.

Henry was now free to march on toward Calais with the brave army that had wellnigh forgotten its weariness in the joy of victory.

THE BATTLE OF AGINCOURT

On the way a halt was called, and the king sent bread and wine to his prisoner, the Duke of Orleans. But the duke, though wounded and faint, refused to eat or drink. Then Henry himself went to see him, and begged him to eat, but still the prisoner refused, saying he wished to fast.

"Cousin," said the king, "make good cheer. If God has granted me grace to gain the victory, I know it is not owing to my deserts. I believe that God wished to punish the French. And if all I have heard is true, it is no wonder, for, they say, never were seen disorders and sins like what are going on in France just now. Surely God did well to be angry."

A little later King Henry reached Calais and sailed for England, where he and his victorious army were greeted with great joy by the citizens of London.

CHAPTER XXXVI

THE BABY-KING OF FRANCE

Soon after the battle of Agincourt the dauphin died; then the king's second son, John, also died—of poison, people whispered. Prince John had been a friend of the Duke of Burgundy, and that alone was enough to make people mutter that the prince had been poisoned by the Armagnacs. They would certainly see to it that no friend of the Burgundian should rule over France.

Charles, the king's youngest son, a boy of fourteen, now became Dauphin. He was an Armagnac, and as this party was the most powerful at the time, all was well with him. The Count of Armagnac took the title of Constable, and ruled France for the young prince.

One of the count's first acts was to imprison Queen Isabelle, who by her wicked conduct did much harm to the kingdom. In 1417, however, she escaped by the help of John, Duke of Burgundy, and from that day she used all her influence on the side of the Burgundians.

The constable ruled Paris better than it had been ruled for years, yet his hand was an iron hand, and before long the citizens grew angry because the count was so stern and showed so little pity. Fickle as ever, they began to think that perhaps after all Queen Isabelle and the Burgundians might prove more gentle rulers.

So in 1418 the citizens opened the gates of Paris to the Burgundians, who poured into the city and slew the Armagnacs, sparing neither women nor little children. The constable was brutally torn to pieces by the angry

THE BABY-KING OF FRANCE 195

mob, and Charles the Dauphin barely escaped with his life.

The Duke of Burgundy had not been with his followers when they entered Paris. As soon as he heard of their violence and the fury of the citizens, he hastened to the capital, but too late to do much good, even had he tried.

Henry v. meanwhile had again come to France with an army, and was besieging the town of Rouen.

John, Duke of Burgundy, who was now ruler of Paris, if not of France, sent an army to relieve the city, but after three months it fell into the hands of the English. Henry at once hastened towards the capital. Then at length the Duke of Burgundy, for the sake of his country, put aside his feud with the Armagnacs. He determined to join them and the dauphin, that together they might save France from falling into the hands of the English and being ruled by an English king.

The dauphin was but a boy, and when he heard that the Duke of Burgundy wished to make peace with him, he did as his courtiers advised. He asked John the Fearless to meet him, that they might discuss their plans together, at the bridge of Montereau, which crossed the river Seine.

Duke John agreed to go to Montereau. Accordingly, a wooden enclosure was built on the middle of the bridge, in which the dauphin and the duke might meet.

Usually a barrier was placed within such an enclosure, lest by any chance a quarrel should arise and swords should thoughtlessly be drawn. At Montereau, alas, no barrier was erected.

A sense of foreboding was heavy upon the followers of the duke. They entreated him not to meet the dauphin; they warned him that the Armagnacs were not to be trusted. Suppose he was taken prisoner, suppose they should attempt to take his life?

But the duke laughed at their fears, or pretended to do so.

"It is my duty," he told his followers, "to risk my person in order to get so great a blessing as peace. Peace being made, I will take the men of my lord the dauphin to go and fight the English."

In July 1419 the meeting at length took place. The dauphin, it was easy to see, had been encouraged by his advisers to be angry. Almost at once when he saw the duke, Charles began to reproach him for not coming earlier to Montereau. He accused him of allowing the English to reach Paris, and many other complaints he made against the man who had risked his life that his country might be saved.

"You have been wanting in your duty," said the dauphin.

"My lord," answered the duke, "I have done only what it was my duty to do."

But still Charles continued to upbraid him, when suddenly one of the Armagnacs who was with the dauphin raised his battle-ax and struck the duke to the ground.

All was at once in confusion. The dauphin hastily withdrew, but the Armagnacs who had been waiting at one side of the bridge now rushed across to the other side where the Burgundians were expecting their master, and soon put them to flight.

Thus after many years the cruel murder of Louis, Duke of Orleans, was avenged upon the noble Duke John the Fearless, who, whatever his faults, had at least loved his country enough to risk his life for her sake.

Philip, the son of John the Fearless, now became Duke of Burgundy. He determined to avenge his father's death, and at once began to fight against the Armagnacs. He also, along with Queen Isabelle, allied himself with the English.

The people of Paris were as eager as the new Duke of Burgundy to have nothing to do with the dauphin or his chosen friends the Armagnacs. The crime they had committed made the citizens wish rather to have Henry, King

THE BABY-KING OF FRANCE 197

of England, to rule over them than the Dauphin and his evil counselors.

Henry was not slow to seize the favorable moment to enter into a treaty with the citizens of Paris.

So the important Treaty of Troyes was signed on May 21, 1420. It declared that on the death of the poor mad king Charles VI., Henry V. of England should become King of France. It also said among other things that Henry should at once marry Catherine, the daughter of Charles VI.

On June 2, 1420, Henry V. therefore entered Paris, and was married to Catherine.

For two years the king and queen held their court in the capital, and during these years Henry ruled justly and well, and restored order to the city, and in part at least to France.

But in August, 1422, Henry V. died, leaving behind him a little son, nine months old, who was also named Henry.

Less than two months later, Charles VI., the poor mad King of France, also died.

While his body lay in state many of his subjects went to lament over him. Their love for Charles had never failed.

"Ah, dear prince," they cried, "never shall we have any so good as thou wert; never shall we see thee more. Since thou dost leave us, we shall never have aught but wars and troubles. As for thee, thou goest to thy rest; as for us, we remain in tribulation and sorrow."

When the service at the tomb of Charles VI. was ended, English heralds proclaimed the tiny baby boy, son of Henry V., King of France and England.

But as the little king, Henry VI., would not be able to rule for many a long year to come, his uncle, the Duke of Bedford, became regent, and ruled France for his little nephew.

Six days after his father's death, Charles the Dauphin also took the title of King, going to the chapel of Mehun,

that he might begin
of the priests.

There were now
baby-king of Paris,
as the French called
of France.

The north of the
and the Burgundians,
was loyal to the daup

In the next chap
which Charles the D
King, not only of
France.

CHAPTER XXXVII

THE SIEGE OF ORLEANS

You have already heard a little about Charles when he was the dauphin, but listen now to what an old chronicler writes of him after he had become king.

"Charles VII," he says, "was a handsome prince, and compassionate toward poor folk; but he did not readily put on his harness, and he had no heart for war if he could do without it." By "harness" the chronicler meant "armor."

It was the greatest pity in the world that Charles VII. had "no heart for war," for war was inevitable if the English were to be turned out of the country, and Charles was ever to claim his true inheritance as King of France.

But as in truth he had "no heart for war," the King of Bourges wandered aimlessly about France, with only a few attendants, sometimes fleeing before the English, sometimes forced to fight them with what army he could collect from his loyal subjects in the south.

It was not only the English who stood in Charles's way, but their allies the Burgundians, without whose help the English would have been too weak to hold France for their baby-king.

Queen Isabelle, the dauphin's mother, had, you remember, also joined the Burgundians, and she did nothing to help her son's cause.

Charles was in a miserable condition. Sometimes he had not even enough money to pay for a pair of boots. He was so unhappy that he often dreamed that he could not really be the king's son, and the true heir to the throne,